ETHICS

G. E. MOORE

OXFORD UNIVERSITY PRESS
London   Oxford   New York

OXFORD UNIVERSITY PRESS

Oxford   London   New York
Glasgow   Toronto   Melbourne   Wellington
Cape Town   Salisbury   Ibadan   Nairobi   Lusaka   Addis Ababa
Bombay   Calcutta   Madras   Karachi   Lahore   Dacca
Kuala Lumpur   Hong Kong   Tokyo

First published, 1912
First issued as an Oxford University Press paperback, 1965

This reprint, 1971

Printed in the United States of America

CONTENTS

I   UTILITARIANISM

Ethics is a subject about which there has been and still is an immense amount of difference of opinion, in spite of all the time and labour which have been devoted to the study of it. There are indeed certain matters about which there is not much disagreement. Almost everybody is agreed that certain kinds of actions ought, as a general rule, to be avoided; and that under certain circumstances, which constantly recur, it is, as a general rule, better to act in certain specified ways rather than in others. There is, moreover, a pretty general agreement, with regard to certain things which happen in the world, that it would be better if they never happened, or, at least, did not happen so often as they do; and with regard to others, that it would be better if they happened more often than they do. But on many questions, even of this kind, there is great diversity of opinion. Actions which some philosophers hold to be generally wrong, others hold to be generally right, and occurrences which some hold to be evils, others hold to be goods.

And when we come to more fundamental questions the difference of opinion is even more marked. Ethical philosophers have, in fact, been largely concerned, not with laying down rules to the effect that certain ways of acting are generally or always right, and others generally or always wrong, nor yet with giving lists of things which are good and others which are evil, but with trying to answer more general and fundamental questions such as the following. What, after all, is it that we mean to say of an action when we say that it is right or ought to be done? And what is it that we mean to say of a state of things when we say that it is good or bad? Can we discover any general characteristic, which belongs in common to absolutely *all* right actions, no matter how different they may be in other respects? and which does not belong to any actions except those which are right? And can we similarly discover any characteristic which belongs in common to absolutely all 'good' things, and which does not belong to any thing except what is a good? Or again, can we discover any single reason, applicable to all right actions equally, which is, in every case, *the* reason why an action is right, when it is right? And can we, similarly, discover any reason which is *the* reason why a thing is good, when it is good, and which also gives us the reason why any one thing is better than another, when it is better? Or is there, perhaps, no such single reason in either case? On questions of this sort different philosophers still hold the most diverse opinions. I think it is true that absolutely every answer which has ever been given to them by any one philosopher would be denied to be true by many others. There is, at any rate, no such consensus of opinion among experts about these fundamental ethical questions, as there is about many fundamental propositions in Mathematics and the Natural Sciences.

Now, it is precisely questions of this sort, about every one of which there are serious differences of opinion, that I wish to discuss in this book. And from the fact that so much difference of opinion exists about them it is natural to infer that they are questions about which it is extremely difficult to discover the truth. This is, I think, really the case. The probability is, that hardly any positive proposition, which can as yet be offered in answer to them, will be strictly and absolutely true. With regard to *negative* propositions, indeed,—propositions to the effect that certain positive answers which have been offered, are false,—the case seems to be different. We are, I think, justified in being much more certain that some of the positive suggestions which have been made are *not* true, than that any particular one among them *is* true; though even here, perhaps, we are not justified in being *absolutely* certain.

But even if we cannot be justified either in accepting or rejecting, with absolute certainty, any of the alternative hypotheses which can be suggested, it is, I think, well worth while to consider carefully the most important among these rival hypotheses. To realize and distinguish clearly from one another the most important of the different views which may be held about these matters is well worth doing, even if we ought to admit that the best of them has no more than a certain amount of probability in its favour, and that the worst have just a possibility of being true. This, therefore, is what I shall try to do. I shall try to state and distinguish clearly from one another what seem to me to be the most important of the different views which may be held upon a few of the most fundamental ethical questions. Some of these views seem to me to be much nearer the truth than others, and I shall try to indicate which these are. But even where it seems pretty certain that some one view is erroneous, and that another comes, at least, rather nearer to the truth, it is very difficult to be sure that the latter is strictly and absolutely true.

One great difficulty which arises in ethical discussions is the difficulty of getting quite clear as to exactly what question it is that we want to answer. And in order to minimize this difficulty, I propose to begin, in these first two chapters, by stating one particular theory, which seems to me to be peculiarly simple and easy to understand. It is a theory which, so far as I can see, comes very near to the truth in some respects, but is quite false in others. And why I propose to begin with it is merely because I think it brings out particularly clearly the difference between several quite distinct questions, which are liable to be confused with one another. If, after stating this theory, we then go on to consider the most important objections which might be urged against it, for various reasons, we shall, I think, pretty well cover the main topics of ethical discussion, so far as fundamental principles are concerned.

This theory starts from the familiar fact that we all very often seem to have a choice between several different actions, any one of which we might do, if we chose. Whether, in such cases, we really do have a choice, in the sense that we ever really *could* choose any other action than the one which in the end we do choose, is a question upon which it does not pronounce and which will have to be considered later on. All that the theory assumes is that, in many cases, there certainly are a considerable number of different actions, any one of which we could do, *if* we chose, and between which, therefore, in *this* sense, we have a choice; while there are others which we could not do, even if we did choose to do them. It assumes, that is to say, that in many cases, *if* we had chosen differently, we should have acted differently; and this seems to be an unquestionable fact, which must be admitted, even if we hold that it is never the case that we *could* have chosen differently. Our theory assumes, then, that many of our actions are under the control of our wills, in the sense that *if*, just before we began to do them, we had chosen not to do them, we *should* not have done them; and I propose to call all actions of this kind *voluntary* actions.

It should be noticed that, if we define voluntary actions in this way, it is by no means certain that all or nearly all voluntary actions are actually themselves chosen or willed. It seems highly probable that an immense number of the actions which we do, and which we *could* have avoided, *if* we had chosen to avoid them, were not themselves willed at all. It is only true of them that they are 'voluntary' in the sense that a particular act of will, just before their occurrence, would have been sufficient to *prevent* them; not in the sense that they themselves were brought about by being willed. And perhaps there is some departure from common usage in calling all such acts 'voluntary'. I do not think, however, that it is in accordance with common usage to restrict the name 'voluntary' to actions which are quite certainly actually willed. And the class of actions to which I propose to give the name—all those, namely, which we could have prevented, *if*, immediately beforehand, we had willed to do so—do, I think, certainly require to be distinguished by some special name. It might, perhaps, be thought that almost all our actions, or even, in a sense, *absolutely* all those, which properly deserve to be called 'ours', are 'voluntary' in this sense: so that the use of this special name is unnecessary: we might, instead, talk simply of 'our actions'. And it is, I think, true that almost all the actions, of which we should generally think, when we talk of 'our actions', are of this nature; and even that, in some contexts, when we talk of 'human actions', we do refer exclusively to actions of this sort. But in other contexts such a way of speaking would be misleading. It is quite certain that both our bodies and our minds constantly do things, which we certainly could not have prevented, by merely willing just beforehand that they should not be done; and some, at least, of these things, which our bodies and minds do, would in certain contexts be called actions of ours. There would therefore be some risk of confusion if we were to speak of 'human actions' generally, when we mean actions which are 'voluntary' in the sense I have defined. It is better, therefore, to give some special name to actions of this class; and I cannot think of any better name than that of 'voluntary' actions. If we require further to distinguish from among them, those which are also voluntary in the sense that we definitely willed to do them, we can do so by calling these 'willed' actions.

Our theory holds, then, that a great many of our actions are voluntary in the sense that we could have avoided them, *if,* just beforehand, we had chosen to do so. It does not pretend to decide whether we *could* have thus chosen to avoid them; it only says that, *if* we had so chosen, we should have succeeded. And its first concern is to lay down some absolutely universal rules as to the conditions under which actions of this kind are *right* or *wrong;* under which they *ought* or *ought not* to be done; and under which it is our *duty* to do them or not to do them. It is quite certain that we do hold that many voluntary actions are right and others wrong; that many ought to have been done, and others ought not to have been done; and that it was the agent's duty to do some of them, and his duty not to do others. Whether any actions, except voluntary ones, can be properly said to be right or wrong, or to be actions which ought or ought not to have been done, and, if so, in what sense and under what conditions, is again a question which our theory does not presume to answer. It only assumes that these things *can* be properly said of some voluntary actions, whether or not they can also be said of other actions as well. It confines itself, therefore, strictly to voluntary actions; and with regard to these it asks the following questions. Can we discover any characteristic, over and above the mere fact that they *are* right, which belongs to absolutely *all* voluntary actions which are right, and which at the same time does not belong to any except those which are right? And similarly: Can we discover any characteristic, over and above the mere fact that they are wrong, which belongs to absolutely *all* voluntary actions which are wrong, and which at the same time does not belong to any except those which are wrong? And so, too, in the case of the words 'ought' and 'duty', it wants to discover some characteristic which belongs to *all* voluntary actions which *ought* to be done or which it is our duty to do, and which does not belong to any except those which we ought to do; and similarly to discover some characteristic which belongs to *all* voluntary actions which ought *not* to be done and which it is our duty *not* to do, and which does not belong to any except these. To all these questions our theory thinks that it can find a comparatively simple answer. And it is this answer which forms the first part of the theory. It is, as I say, a *comparatively* simple answer; but nevertheless it cannot be stated accurately except at some length. And I think it is worth while to try to state it accurately.

To begin with, then, this theory points out that all actions may, theoretically at least, be arranged in a scale, according to the proportion between the *total* quantities of pleasure or pain which they *cause*. And when it talks of the *total* quantities of pleasure or pain which an action causes, it is extremely important to realize that it means quite strictly what it says. We all of us know that many of our actions do cause pleasure and pain not only to ourselves, but also to other human beings, and sometimes, perhaps, to animals as well; and that the effects of our actions, in this respect, are often not confined to those which are comparatively direct and immediate, but that their indirect and remote effects are sometimes quite equally important or even more so. But in order to arrive at the *total* quantities of pleasure or pain caused by an action, we should, of course, have to take into account absolutely *all* its effects, both near and remote, direct and indirect; and we should have to take into account absolutely *all* the beings, capable of feeling pleasure or pain, who were at any time affected by it; not only ourselves, therefore, and our fellow-men, but also any of the lower animals, to which the action might cause pleasure or pain, however indirectly; and also any other beings in the Universe, if there should be any, who might be affected in the same way. Some people, for instance, hold that there is a God and that there are disembodied spirits, who may be pleased or pained by our actions; and, if this is so, then, in order to arrive at the *total* quantities of pleasure or pain which an action causes, we should have, of course, to take into account, not only the pleasures or pains which it may cause to men and animals upon this earth, but also those which it may cause to God or to disembodied spirits. By the *total* quantities of pleasure or pain which an action causes, this theory means, then, quite strictly what it says. It means the quantities which would be arrived at, if we could take into account absolutely *all* the amounts of pleasure or pain, which result from the action; no matter how indirect or remote these results may be, and no matter what may be the nature of the beings who feel them.

But if we understand the total quantities of pleasure or pain caused by an action in this strict sense, then obviously, theoretically at least, six different cases are possible. It is obviously theoretically possible in the first place (1) that an action should, in its total effects, cause some pleasure but absolutely no pain; and it is obviously also possible

(2) that, while it causes both pleasure and pain, the total quantity of pleasure should be *greater* than the total quantity of pain. These are two out of the six theoretically possible cases; and these two may be grouped together by saying that, in both of them, the action in question causes an *excess* of pleasure over pain, or *more* pleasure than pain. This description will, of course, if taken quite strictly, apply only to the second of the two; since an action which causes no pain whatever cannot strictly be said to cause more pleasure than pain. But it is convenient to have some description, which may be understood to cover both cases; and if we describe no pain at all as a *zero* quantity of pain, then obviously we may say that an action which causes some pleasure and no pain, does cause a *greater* quantity of pleasure than of pain, since any positive quantity is greater than zero. I propose, therefore, for the sake of convenience, to speak of both these first two cases as cases in which an action causes an *excess* of pleasure over pain.

But obviously two other cases, which are also theoretically possible, are (1) that in which an action, in its total effects, causes some pain but absolutely no pleasure, and (2) that in which, while it causes both pleasure and pain, the total quantity of *pain* is greater than the total quantity of *pleasure*. And of both these two cases I propose to speak, for the reason just explained, as cases in which an action causes an *excess* of *pain* over *pleasure*.

There remain two other cases, and two only, which are still theoretically possible; namely (1) that an action should cause absolutely no pleasure and also absolutely no pain, and (2) that, while it causes both pleasure and pain, the total quantities of each should be exactly equal. And in both these two cases, we may, of course, say that the action in question causes *no* excess either of pleasure over pain or of pain over pleasure.

Of absolutely every action, therefore, it must be true, in the sense explained, that it either causes an excess of pleasure over pain, or an excess of pain over pleasure, or neither. This threefold division covers all the six possible cases. But, of course, of any two actions, both of which cause an excess of pleasure over pain, or of pain over pleasure, it may be true that the excess caused by the one is *greater* than that caused by the other. And, this being so, all actions may, theoretically at least, be arranged in a scale, starting at the top with those which cause the *greatest* excess of pleasure over pain; passing downwards by degrees through cases where the excess of pleasure over pain is continually smaller and smaller, until we reach those actions which cause no excess either of pleasure over pain or of pain over pleasure: then starting again with those which cause an excess of pain over pleasure, but only the smallest possible one; going on by degrees to cases in which the excess of pain over pleasure is continually larger and larger; until we reach, at the bottom, those cases in which the excess of pain over pleasure is the greatest.

The principle upon which this scale is arranged is, I think, perfectly easy to understand, though it cannot be stated accurately except in rather a complicated way. The principle is: That any action which causes an excess of pleasure over pain will always come higher in the scale *either* than an action which causes a *smaller* excess of pleasure over pain, *or* than an action which causes no excess either of pleasure over pain or of pain over pleasure, *or* than one which causes an excess of pain over pleasure; That any action which causes no excess either of pleasure over pain or of pain over pleasure will always come higher than any which causes an excess of pain over pleasure; and finally That any, which causes an excess of pain over pleasure, will always come higher than one which causes a *greater* excess of pain over pleasure. And obviously this statement is rather complicated. But yet, so far as I can see, there is no simpler way of stating quite accurately the principle upon which the scale is arranged. By saying that one action comes higher in the scale than another, we may mean any one of these five different things; and I can find no simple expression which will really apply quite accurately to all five cases.

But it has, I think, been customary, among ethical writers, to speak loosely of any action, which comes higher in this scale than another, for any one of these five reasons, as causing *more* pleasure than that other, or causing a *greater balance* of pleasure over pain. For instance, if we are comparing five different actions, one of which comes higher in the scale than any of the rest, it has been customary to say that, among the five, this is the one which causes a *maximum* of pleasure, or a *maximum balance* of pleasure over pain. To speak in this way is obviously extremely inaccurate, for many different reasons. It is obvious, for instance, that an action which comes lower in the scale may actually produce much more pleasure than one which comes higher, provided this effect is counteracted by its *also* causing a much greater quantity of pain. And it is obvious also that, of two actions, one of which comes higher in the scale than another, *neither* may cause a balance of pleasure over pain, but both actually more pain than pleasure. For these and other reasons it is quite inaccurate to speak as if the place of an action in the scale were determined either by the total quantity of pleasure that it causes, or by the total balance of pleasure over pain. But this way of speaking, though inaccurate, is also extremely convenient; and of the two alternative expressions, the one which is the most inaccurate is also the most convenient. It is much more convenient to be able to refer to any action which comes higher in the scale as simply causing *more pleasure,* than to have to say, every time, that it causes *a greater balance of pleasure over pain.*

I propose, therefore, in spite of its inaccuracy, to adopt this loose way of speaking. And I do not think the adoption of it need lead to any confusion, provided it is clearly understood, to begin with, that I am going to use the words in this loose way. It must, therefore, be clearly understood that, when, in what follows, I speak of one action as causing more pleasure than another, I shall not mean strictly what I say, but only that the former action is related to the latter in one or other of the five following ways. I shall mean that the two actions are related to one another either (1) by the fact that, while both cause an excess of pleasure over pain, the former causes a greater excess than the latter; or (2) by the fact that, while the former causes an excess of pleasure over pain, the latter causes no excess whatever either of pleasure over pain, or of pain over pleasure; or (3) by the fact that, while the former causes an excess of pleasure over pain, the latter causes an excess of pain over pleasure; or (4) by the fact that, while the former causes no excess whatever either of pleasure over pain or of pain over pleasure, the latter does cause an excess of pain over pleasure; or (5) by the fact that, while both cause an excess of pain over pleasure, the former causes a smaller excess than the latter. It must be remembered, too, that in every case we shall be speaking of the *total* quantities of pleasure and pain caused by the actions, in the strictest possible sense; taking into account, that is to say, absolutely *all* their effects, however remote and indirect.

But now, if we understand the statement that one action causes more pleasure than another in the sense just explained, we may express as follows the first principle, which the theory I wish to state lays down with regard to right and wrong, as applied to voluntary actions. This first principle is a very simple one; for it merely asserts: That a voluntary action is right, whenever and only when the agent could *not,* even if he had chosen, have done any other action instead, which would have caused more pleasure than the one he did do; and that a voluntary action is wrong, whenever and only when the agent *could,* if he had chosen, have done some other action instead, which would have caused more pleasure than the one he did do. It must be remembered that our theory does not assert that any agent ever could have *chosen* any other action than the one he actually performed. It only asserts, that, in the case of all voluntary actions, he *could* have acted differently, *if* he had chosen: not that he could have made the choice. It does not assert, therefore, that right and wrong depend upon what he could *choose.* As to this, it makes no assertion at all: it neither affirms nor denies that they do so depend. It only asserts that they do depend upon what he could have done or could do, *if* he chose. In every case of voluntary action, a man could, *if* he had so chosen just before, have done at least one other action instead. That was the definition of a voluntary action: and it seems quite certain that many actions are voluntary in this sense. And what our theory asserts is that, where among the actions which he could thus have done instead, *if* he had chosen, there is any one which would have caused more pleasure than the one he did do, then his action is always wrong; but that in all other cases it is right. This is what our theory asserts, if we remember that the phrase 'causing more pleasure' is to be understood in the inaccurate sense explained above.

But it will be convenient, in what follows, to introduce yet another inaccuracy in our statement of it. It asserts, we have seen, that the question whether a voluntary action is right or wrong, depends upon the question whether, among all the other actions, which the agent could have done instead, *if* he had chosen, there is or is not any which would have produced more pleasure than the one he did do. But it would be highly inconvenient, every time we have to mention the theory, to use the whole phrase 'all the other actions which the agent could have done instead, *if* he had chosen'. I propose, therefore, instead to call these simply 'all the other actions which he *could* have done', or 'which were possible to him'. This is, of course, inaccurate, since it is, in a sense, not true that he *could* have done them, if he could not have chosen them: and our theory does not pretend to say whether he *ever* could have chosen them. Moreover, even if it is true that he could *sometimes* have chosen an action which he did not choose, it is pretty certain that it is not always so; it is pretty certain that it is *sometimes* out of his power to choose an action, which he certainly could have done, *if* he had chosen. It is not true, therefore, that *all* the actions which he could have done, *if* he had chosen, are actions which, in every sense, he *could* have done, even if it is true that some of them are. But nevertheless I propose, for the sake of brevity, to speak of them all as actions which he *could* have done; and this again, I think, need lead to no confusion, if it be clearly understood that I am doing so. It must, then, be clearly understood that, when, in what follows, I speak of all the actions which the agent could have done, or all those open to him under the circumstances, I shall mean only all those which he could have done, *if* he had chosen.

Understanding this, then, we may state the first principle which our theory lays down quite briefly by saying: 'A voluntary action is right, whenever and only when no other action possible to the agent under the circumstances would have caused more pleasure; in all other cases, it is wrong.' This is its answer to the questions: What characteristic is there which belongs to *all* voluntary actions which are right, and *only* those among them which are right? and what characteristic is there which belongs to *all* those which are wrong, and *only* to those which are wrong? But it also asked the very same questions with regard to two other classes of voluntary actions—those which *ought* or ought *not* to be done, and those which it is our *duty* to do or not to do. And its answer to the question concerning these conceptions differs from its answer to the question concerning right and wrong in a way, which is, indeed, comparatively unimportant, but which yet deserves to be noticed.

It may have been observed that our theory does *not* assert that a voluntary action is right only where it causes *more* pleasure than any action which the agent could have done instead. It confines itself to asserting that, in order to be right, such an action must cause at least as *much* pleasure as any which the agent could have done instead. And it confines itself in this way for the following reason. It is obviously possible, theoretically at least, that, among the alternatives open to an agent at a given moment, there may be two or more which would produce precisely *equal* amounts of pleasure, while all of them produced more than any of the other possible alternatives; and in such cases, our theory would say, *any one* of these actions would be perfectly right. It recognizes, therefore, that there may be cases in which no single one of the actions open to the agent can be distinguished as *the* right one to do; that in many cases, on the contrary, several different actions may all be equally right; or, in other words, that to say that a man acted rightly does not necessarily imply that, if he had done anything else instead, he would have acted wrongly. And this is certainly in accordance with common usage. We all do constantly imply that sometimes when a man was right in doing what he did, yet he might have been equally right, if he had acted differently: that there may be several different alternatives open to him, none of which can definitely be said to be wrong. This is why our theory refuses to commit itself to the view that an action is right only where it produces *more* pleasure than any of the other possible alternatives. For, if this were so, then it would follow that no two alternatives could ever be *equally* right: some one of them would always have to be *the* right one, and all the rest wrong. But it is precisely in this respect that it holds that the conceptions of 'ought' and of 'duty' differ from the conception of what is 'right'. When we say that a man 'ought' to do one particular action, or that it is his 'duty' to do it, we do imply that it would be wrong for him to do *anything* else. And hence our theory holds that, in the case of 'ought' and 'duty' we may say, what we could not say in the case of 'right', namely, that an action ought to be done or is our duty, only where it produces *more* pleasure than any which we could have done instead.

From this distinction several consequences follow. It follows firstly that a voluntary action may be 'right' without being an action which we 'ought' to do or which it is our 'duty' to do. It is, of course, always our duty to act rightly, in the sense that, if we don't act rightly, we shall always be doing what we ought not. It is, therefore, true, in a sense, that whenever we act rightly, we are always doing our duty and doing what we ought. But what is not true is that, whenever a particular action is right, it is always our duty to do that particular action and no other. This is not true, because, theoretically at least, cases may occur in which some other action would be quite equally right, and in such cases, we are obviously under no obligation whatever to do the one rather than the other: whichever we do, we shall be doing our duty and doing as we ought. And it would be rash to affirm that such cases never do practically occur. We all commonly hold that they do: that very often indeed we are under no positive obligation to do one action rather than some other; that it does not matter which we do. We must, then, be careful not to affirm that, because it is always our duty to act rightly, therefore any particular action, which is right, is always also one which it is our duty to do. This is not so, because, even where an action is right, it does not follow that it would be wrong to do something else instead; whereas, if an action is a duty or an action which we positively ought to do, it always would be wrong to do anything else instead.

The first consequence, then, which follows, from this distinction between what is right, on the one hand, and what ought to be done or is our duty, on the other, is that a voluntary action may be right, without being an action which we ought to do or which it is our duty to do. And from this it follows further that the relation between 'right' and what ought to be done is not on a par with that between 'wrong' and what ought *not* to be done. Every action which is wrong is also an action which ought not to be done and which it is our duty not to do; and also, conversely, every action which ought not to be done, or which it is our duty not to do, is wrong. These three negative terms are precisely and absolutely coextensive. To say that an action is or was wrong, is to imply that it ought not to be, or to have been, done; and the converse implication also holds. But in the case of 'right' and 'ought', only one of the two converse propositions holds. Every action which ought to be done or which is our duty, is certainly also right; to say the one thing of any action is to imply the other. But here the converse is not true; since, as we have seen, to say that an action is right is *not* to imply that it ought to be done or that it is our duty: an action may be right, without either of these two other things being true of it. In this respect the relation between the positive conceptions 'right' and 'ought to be done' is not on a par with that between the negative conceptions 'wrong' and 'ought not to be done'. The two positive conceptions are not coextensive, whereas the two negative ones are so.

And thirdly and finally, it also follows that whereas every voluntary action, without exception, must be either right or wrong, it is by no means necessarily true of every voluntary action that it either ought to be done or ought not to be done,—that it either is our duty to do it, or our duty not to do it. On the contrary, cases may occur quite frequently where it is neither our duty to do a particular action, nor yet our duty not to do it. This will occur, whenever, among the alternatives open to us, there are two or more, any one of which would be equally right. And hence we must not suppose that, wherever we have a choice of actions before us, there is always some one among them (*if* we could only find out which), which is *the* one which we ought to do, while all the rest are definitely wrong. It may quite well be the case that there is no one among them, which we are under a positive obligation to do, although there always must be at least one which it would be right to do. There will be one which we definitely *ought* to do, in those cases and those cases only, where there happens to be *only* one which is right under the circumstances—where, that is to say, there are not several which would all be equally right, but some one of the alternatives open to us is *the* only right thing to do. And hence in many cases we cannot definitely say of a voluntary action either that it was the agent's duty to do it nor yet that it was his duty not to do it. There may be cases in which none of the alternatives open to us is definitely prescribed by duty.

To sum up, then: The answers which this theory gives to its first set of questions is as follows. A characteristic which belongs to all right voluntary actions, and only to those which are right, is, it says, this: That they all cause at least *as much* pleasure as any action which the agent could have done instead; or, in other words, they all produce *a* maximum of pleasure. A characteristic which belongs to all voluntary actions, which *ought* to be done or which it is our *duty* to do, and only to these, is, it says, the slightly different one: That they all cause *more* pleasure than any which the agent could have done instead; or, in other words, among all the possible alternatives, it is they which produce *the* maximum of pleasure. And finally, a characteristic which belongs to all voluntary actions which are wrong, or which ought not to be done, or which it is our duty not to do, and which belongs only to these, is, in all three cases the same, namely: That they all cause *less* pleasure than some other action which the agent could have done instead. These three statements together constitute what I will call the first part of the theory; and, whether we agree with them or not, it must, I think, at least be admitted that they are propositions of a very fundamental nature and of a very wide range, so that it would be worth while to know, if possible, whether they are true.

But this first part of the theory is by no means the whole of it. There are two other parts of it, which are at least equally important; and, before we go on to consider the objections which may be urged against it, it will, I think, be best to state these other parts. They may, however, conveniently form the subject of a new chapter.

In the last chapter I stated the first part of an ethical theory, which I chose out for consideration, not because I agreed with it, but because it seemed to me to bring out particularly clearly the distinction between some of the most fundamental subjects of ethical discussion. This first part consisted in asserting that there is a certain characteristic which belongs to absolutely *all* voluntary actions which are right, and *only* to those which are right; another closely allied characteristic which belongs to *all* voluntary actions which ought to be done or are duties, and *only* to these; a third characteristic which belongs to *all* voluntary actions which are wrong, ought not to be done, or which it is our duty not to do, and *only* to those voluntary actions of which these things are true. And when the theory makes these assertions it means the words 'all' and 'only' to be understood quite strictly. That is to say, it means its propositions to apply to absolutely every voluntary action, which ever has been done, or ever will be done, no matter who did it, or when it was or will be done; and not only to those which actually have been or will be done, but also to all those which have been or will be *possible,* in a certain definite sense.

The sense in which it means its propositions to apply to *possible,* as well as actual, voluntary actions, is, it must be remembered, only if we agree to give the name 'possible' to all those actions which an agent *could* have done, *if* he had chosen, and to those which, in the future, any agent will be able to do, *if* he were to choose to do them. Possible actions, in this sense, form a perfectly definite group; and we do, as a matter of fact, often make judgements as to whether they would have been or would be right, and as to whether they ought to have been done in the past, or ought to be done in the future. We say, 'So-and-so ought to have done this on that occasion', or 'It would have been perfectly right for him to have done this', although as a matter of fact, he did not do it; or we say, 'You ought to do this', or 'It will be quite right for you to do this', although it subsequently turns out, that the action in question is one which you do not actually perform. Our theory says, then, with regard to all actions, which were in this sense possible in the past, that they *would have been* right, if and only if they *would* have produced a maximum of pleasure; just as it says that all actual past voluntary actions *were* right, if and only if they *did* produce a maximum of pleasure. And similarly, with regard to all voluntary actions which will be possible in the future, it says that they will be right, if and only if they *would* produce a maximum of pleasure; just as it says with regard to all that will actually be done, that they will be right, if and only if they *do* produce a maximum of pleasure.

Our theory does, then, even in its first part, deal, in a sense, with possible actions, as well as actual ones. It professes to tell us, not only which among actual past voluntary actions *were* right, but also which among those which were possible *would have been* right if they had been done; and not only which among the voluntary actions which actually will be done in the future, *will* be right, but also which among those which will be possible, *would* be right, if they *were* to be done. And in doing this, it does, of course, give us a criterion, or test, or standard, by means of which we could, theoretically at least, discover with regard to absolutely every voluntary action, whichever either has been or will be either actual or possible, whether it was or will be right or not. If we want to discover with regard to a voluntary action which was actually done or was possible in the past, whether it was right or would have been right, we have only to ask: Could the agent, on the occasion in question, have done anything else instead, which would have produced more pleasure? If he could, then the action in question was or would have been wrong; if he could not, then it was or would have been right. And similarly, if we want to discover with regard to an action, which we are contemplating in the future, whether it would be right for us to do it, we have only to ask: Could I do anything else instead which would produce more pleasure? If I could, it will be wrong to do the action; if I could not, it will be right. Our theory does then, even in its first part, profess to give us an absolutely universal *criterion* of right and wrong; and similarly also an absolutely universal *criterion* of what ought or ought not to be done.

But though it does this, there is something else which it does not do. It only asserts, in this first part, that the producing of a maximum of pleasure is a characteristic, which did and will belong, *as a matter of fact,* to all right voluntary actions (actual or possible), and only to right ones; it does not, in its first part, go on to assert that it is *because* they possess this characteristic that such actions are right. This second assertion is the first which it goes on to make in its second part; and everybody can see, I think, that there is an important difference between the two assertions.

Many people might be inclined to admit that, whenever a man acts wrongly, his action always does, on the whole, result in greater unhappiness than would have ensued if he had acted differently; and that when he acts rightly this result *never* ensues: that, on the contrary, right action always does in the end bring about at least as much happiness, on the whole, as the agent could possibly have brought about by any other action which was in his power. The proposition that wrong action always *does,* and (considering how the Universe is constituted) always *would,* in the long run, lead to less pleasure than the agent could have brought about by acting differently, and that right action never *does* and never *would* have this effect, is a proposition which a great many people might be inclined to accept; and this is all which, in its first part, our theory asserts. But many of those who would be inclined to assent to this proposition, would feel great hesitation in going on to assert that this is *why* actions are right or wrong respectively. There seems to be a very important difference between the two positions. We may hold, for instance, that an act of murder, whenever it is wrong, always does produce greater unhappiness than would have followed if the agent had chosen instead some one of the other alternatives, which he could have carried out, *if* he had so chosen; and we may hold that this is true of all other wrong actions, actual or possible, and never of any right ones: but it seems a very different thing to hold that murder and all other wrong actions are wrong, when they are wrong, *because* they have this result—*because* they produce less than the possible maximum of pleasure. We may hold, that is to say, that the fact that it does produce or would produce *less* than a maximum of pleasure is absolutely always a *sign* that a voluntary action is wrong, while the fact that it does produce or would produce a maximum of pleasure is absolutely always a *sign* that it is right; but this does not seem to commit us to the very different proposition that these results, besides being *signs* of right and wrong, are also the *reasons* why actions are right when they are right, and wrong when they are wrong. Everybody can see, I think, that the distinction is important; although I think it is often overlooked in ethical discussions. And it is precisely this distinction which separates what I have called the first part of our theory, from the first of the assertions which it goes on to make in its second part. In its first part it only asserts that the producing or not producing a maximum of pleasure are, absolutely universally, *signs* of right and wrong in voluntary actions; in its second part it goes on to assert that it is *because* they produce these results that voluntary actions are right when they are right, and wrong when they are wrong.

There is, then, plainly some important difference between the assertion, which our theory made in its first part, to the effect that all right voluntary actions, and only those which are right, do, *in fact,* produce a maximum of pleasure, and the assertion, which it now goes on to make, that this is *why* they are right. And if we ask why the difference is important, the answer is, so far as I can see, as follows. Namely, if we say that actions are right, *because* they produce a maximum of pleasure, we imply that, provided they produced this result, they *would* be right, *no matter what other effects they might produce* as well. We imply, in short, that their rightness does *not* depend at all upon their other effects, but *only* on the quantity of pleasure that they produce. And this is a very different thing from merely saying that the producing a maximum of pleasure is always, as a matter of fact, a *sign* of rightness. It is quite obvious, that, in the Universe as it is actually constituted, pleasure and pain are by no means the only results of any of our actions: they all produce immense numbers of other results as well. And so long as we merely assert that the producing a maximum of pleasure is a *sign* of rightness, we leave open the possibility that it is so only because this result does always, as a matter of fact, happen to coincide with the production of *other* results; but that it is partly upon these other results that the rightness of the action depends. But so soon as we assert that actions are right, *because* they produce a maximum of pleasure, we cut away this possibility; we assert that actions which produced such a maximum *would* be right, even if they did not produce any of the other effects, which, as a matter of fact, they always do produce.

And this, I think, is the chief reason why many persons who would be inclined to assent to the first proposition, would hesitate to assent to the second.

It is, for instance, commonly held that some pleasures are higher or better than others, even though they may not be more pleasant; and that where we have a choice between procuring for ourselves or others a higher or a lower pleasure, it is generally right to prefer the former, even though it may perhaps be less pleasant. And, of course, even those who hold that actions are only right because of the quantity of pleasure they produce, and not at all because of the quality of these pleasures, might quite consistently hold that it is *as a matter of fact* generally right to prefer higher pleasures to lower ones, even though they may be less pleasant. They might hold that this is the case, on the ground that higher pleasures, even when less pleasant in themselves, do, if we take into account all their further effects, tend to produce more pleasure on the whole than lower ones. There is a good deal to be said for the view that this does actually happen, as the Universe is actually constituted; and that hence an action which causes a higher pleasure to be enjoyed instead of a lower one, will in general cause *more* pleasure in its *total* effects, though it may cause *less* in its *immediate* effects. And this is why those who hold that higher pleasures are in general to be preferred to lower ones, may nevertheless admit that mere quantity of pleasure is always, *in fact,* a correct *sign* or *criterion* of the rightness of an action.

But those who hold that actions are only right, *because* of the quantity of pleasure they produce, must hold also that, *if* higher pleasures did not, in their total effects, produce *more* pleasure than lower ones, then there *would* be no reason whatever for preferring them, provided they were not themselves more pleasant. *If* the *sole* effect of one action were to be the enjoyment of a certain amount of the most bestial or idiotic pleasure, and the *sole* effect of another were to be the enjoyment of a much more refined one, then they must hold that there would be no reason whatever for preferring the latter to the former, provided only that the mere quantity of pleasure enjoyed in each case were the same. And if the bestial pleasure were ever so slightly more pleasant than the other, then they must say it would be our positive duty to do the action which would bring it about rather than the other. This is a conclusion which does follow from the assertion that actions are right *because* they produce a maximum of pleasure, and which does not follow from the mere assertion that the producing a maximum of pleasure is always, *in fact*, a sign of rightness. And it is for this, and similar reasons, that it is important to distinguish the two propositions.

To many persons it may seem clear that it *would* be our duty to prefer some pleasures to others, even if they did not entail a greater *quantity* of pleasure; and hence that though actions which produce a maximum of pleasure are perhaps, *in fact*, always right, they are not right *because* of this, but only because the producing of this result does in fact happen to coincide with the producing of other results. They would say that though perhaps, in fact, actual cases never occur in which it *is* or would be wrong to do an action, which produces a maximum of pleasure, it is easy to *imagine* cases in which it *would* be wrong. *If*, for instance, we had to choose between creating a Universe, in which all the inhabitants were capable only of the lowest sensual pleasures, and another in which they were capable of the highest intellectual and aesthetic ones, it would, they would say, plainly be our duty to create the latter rather than the former, even though the mere quantity of pleasure enjoyed in it were rather less than in the former, and still more so if the quantities were equal. Or, to put it shortly, they would say that a world of men is preferable to a world of pigs, even though the pigs might enjoy as much or more pleasure than a world of men. And this is what our theory goes on to deny, when it says that voluntary actions are right, *because* they produce a maximum of pleasure. It implies, by saying this, that actions which produced a maximum of pleasure *would* always be right, no matter what their effects, in other respects, might be. And hence that it *would* be right to create a world in which there was no intelligence and none of the higher emotions, rather than one in which these were present in the highest degree, provided only that the mere quantity of pleasure enjoyed in the former were ever so little greater than that enjoyed in the latter.

Our theory asserts, then, in its second part, that voluntary actions are right when they are right, *because* they produce a maximum of pleasure; and in asserting this it takes a great step beyond what it asserted in its first part, since it now implies that an action which produced a maximum of pleasure always *would* be right, no matter how its results, in other respects, might compare with those of the other possible alternatives.

But it might be held that, even so, it does not imply that this would be so *absolutely unconditionally*. It might be held that though, in the Universe as actually constituted, actions are right *because* they produce a maximum of pleasure, and hence their rightness does not at all depend upon their *other* effects, yet this is only so for some such reason as that, in this Universe, all conscious beings do actually happen to desire pleasure; but that, if we could imagine a Universe, in which pleasure was not desired, then, in such a Universe, actions would *not* be right because they produced a maximum of pleasure; and hence that we cannot lay it down absolutely unconditionally that in all conceivable Universes any voluntary action would be right whenever and only when it produced a maximum of pleasure. For some such reason as this, it might be held that we must distinguish between the mere assertion that voluntary actions are right, when they are right, *because* they produce a maximum of pleasure, and the further assertion that this *would* be so in all conceivable circumstances and in any conceivable Universe. Those who assert the former are by no means necessarily bound to assert the latter also. To assert the latter is to take a still further step.

But the theory I wish to state does, in fact, take this further step. It asserts not only that, in the Universe as it is, voluntary actions are right *because* they produce a maximum of pleasure, but also that this would be so, *under any conceivable circumstances*: that if any conceivable being, in any conceivable Universe, were faced with a choice between an action which would cause more pleasure and one which would cause less, it would *always* be his duty to choose the former rather than the latter, no matter what the respects might be in which his Universe differed from ours. It may, at first sight, seem unduly bold to assert that any ethical truth can be absolutely unconditional in this sense. But many philosophers have held that some fundamental ethical principles certainly are thus unconditional. And a little reflection will suffice to show that the view that they may be so is at all events not absurd. We have many instances of other truths, which seem quite plainly to be of this nature. It seems quite clear, for instance, that it is not only true that twice two do make four, in the Universe as it actually is, but that they necessarily would make four, in any conceivable Universe, no matter how much it might differ from this one in other respects. And our theory is only asserting that the connexion which it believes to hold between rightness and the production of a maximum of pleasure is, in this respect, similar to the connexion asserted to hold between the number two and the number four, when we say that twice two are four. It asserts that, if any being whatever, in any circumstances whatever, had to choose between two actions, one of which would produce more pleasure than the other, it always would be his duty to choose the former rather than the latter: that this is absolutely unconditionally true. This assertion obviously goes very much further, both than the assertion which it made in its first part, to the effect that the producing a maximum of pleasure is a *sign* of rightness in the case of all voluntary actions, that ever have been or will be actual or possible, and also than the assertion, that in the Universe, as it is actually constituted, actions are right, when they are right, *because* they produce a maximum of pleasure. But bold as the assertion may seem, it is, at all events, not impossible that we should know it to be true.

Our theory asserts, therefore, in its second part: That, if we had to choose between two actions, one of which would have as its sole or total effects, an effect or set of effects, which we may call A, while the other would have as its sole or total effects, an effect or set of effects, which we may call B, then, *if* A contained more pleasure than B, it always would be our duty to choose the action which caused A rather than that which caused B. This, it asserts, would be absolutely *always* true, *no matter what A and B might be like in other respects.* And to assert this is (it now goes on to say) *equivalent* to asserting that any effect or set of effects which contains more pleasure is always *intrinsically* better than one which contains less.

By calling one effect or set of effects *intrinsically better* than another it means that it is better *in itself,* quite apart from any accompaniments or further effects which it may have. That is to say: To assert of any one thing, A, that it is *intrinsically* better than another, B, is to assert that if A existed *quite alone,* without any accompaniments or effects whatever—if, in short, A constituted the whole Universe, it would be better that such a Universe should exist, than that a Universe which consisted solely of B should exist instead. In order to discover whether any one thing is *intrinsically* better than another, we have always thus to consider whether it would be better that the one should exist *quite alone* than that the other should exist *quite alone.* No one thing or set of things, A, ever can be *intrinsically* better than another, B, unless it would be better that A should exist quite alone than that B should exist quite alone. Our theory asserts, therefore, that, wherever it is true that it would be our *duty* to choose A rather than B, if A and B were to be the sole effects of a pair of actions between which we had to choose, there it is always also true that it would be *better* that A should exist quite alone than that B should exist quite alone. And it asserts also, conversely, that wherever it is true that any one thing or set of things, A, is intrinsically better than another, B, there it would always also be our duty to choose an action of which A would be the sole effect rather than one of which B would be the sole effect, if we had to choose between them. But since, as we have seen, it holds that it never could be our duty to choose one action rather than another, unless the total effects of the one contained more pleasure than that of the other, it follows that, according to it, no effect or set of effects, A, can possibly be intrinsically better than another, B, *unless* it contains more pleasure. It holds, therefore, not only that any one effect or set of effects, which contains more pleasure, is always intrinsically better than one which contains less, but also that no effect or set of effects can be intrinsically better than another *unless* it contains more pleasure.

It is plain, then, that this theory assigns a quite unique position to pleasure and pain in two respects; or possibly only in one, since it is just possible that the two propositions which it makes about them are not merely equivalent, but absolutely identical—that is to say, are merely different ways of expressing exactly the same idea. The two propositions are these. (1) That if any one had to choose between two actions, one of which would, in its total effects, cause more pleasure than the other, it always would be his duty to choose the former; and that it never could be any one's duty to choose one action rather than another, unless its total effects contained more pleasure. (2) That any Universe, or part of a Universe, which contains more pleasure, is always intrinsically better than one which contains less; and that nothing can be intrinsically better than anything else, unless it contains more pleasure. It does seem to be just possible that these two propositions are merely two different ways of expressing exactly the same idea. The question whether they are so or not simply depends upon the question whether, when we say, 'It would be better that A should exist quite alone than that B should exist quite alone', we are or are not saying exactly the same thing, as when we say, 'Supposing we had to choose between an action of which A would be the sole effect, and one of which B would be the sole effect, it would be our duty to choose the former rather than the latter'. And it certainly does seem, at first sight, as if the two propositions were not identical; as if we should not be saying exactly the same thing in asserting the one, as in asserting the other. But, even if they are not identical, our theory asserts that they are certainly *equivalent*: that, whenever the one is true, the other is certainly also true. And, if they are not identical, this assertion of equivalence amounts to the very important proposition that: An action is right, only if no action, which the agent could have done instead, would have had intrinsically better results: while an action is wrong, only if the agent *could* have done some other action instead whose total results would have been intrinsically better. It certainly seems as if this proposition were not a mere tautology. And, if so, then we must admit that our theory assigns a unique position to pleasure and pain in two respects, and not in one only. It asserts, first of all, that they have a unique relation to right and wrong; and secondly, that they have a unique relation to *intrinsic value*.

Our theory asserts, then, that any whole which contains a greater amount of pleasure, is always intrinsically better than one which contains a smaller amount, no matter what the two may be like in other respects; and that no whole can be intrinsically better than another unless it contains more pleasure. But it must be remembered that throughout this discussion, we have, for the sake of convenience, been using the phrase 'contains more pleasure' in an inaccurate sense. I explained that I should say of one whole, A, that it contained more pleasure than another, B, whenever A and B were related to one another in either of the five following ways: namely (1) when A and B both contain an excess of pleasure over pain, but A contains a greater excess than B; (2) when A contains an excess of pleasure over pain, while B contains no excess either of pleasure over pain or of pain over pleasure; (3) when A contains an excess of pleasure over pain, while B contains an excess of pain over pleasure, (4) when A contains no excess either of pleasure over pain or of pain over pleasure, while B does contain an excess of pain over pleasure; and (5) when both A and B contain an excess of pain over pleasure, but A contains a smaller excess than B. Whenever in stating this theory, I have spoken of one whole, or effect, or set of effects, A, as containing more pleasure than another, B, I have always meant merely that A was related to B *in one or other of these five ways*. And so here, when our theory says that every whole which contains a greater amount of pleasure is always intrinsically better than one which contains less, and that nothing can be intrinsically better than anything else unless it contains more pleasure, this must be understood to mean that any whole, A, which stands to another, B, in *any one* of these five relations, is always intrinsically better than B, and that no one thing can be intrinsically better than another, unless it stands to it in *one or other* of these five relations. And it becomes important to remember this, when we go on to take account of another fact.

It is plain that when we talk of one thing being 'better' than another we may mean any one of five different things. We may mean either (1) that while both are positively good, the first is better; or (2) that while the first is positively good, the second is neither good nor bad, but indifferent; or (3) that while the first is positively good, the second is positively bad; or (4) that while the first is indifferent, the second is positively bad; or (5) that while both are positively bad, the first is less bad than the second. We should, in common life, say that one thing was 'better' than another, whenever it stood to that other in any one of these five relations. Or, in other words, we hold that among things which stand to one another in the relation of better and worse, some are positively good, others positively bad, and others neither good nor bad, but indifferent. And our theory holds that this is, in fact, the case, with things which have a place in the scale of *intrinsic* value: some of them are intrinsically good, others intrinsically bad, and others indifferent. And it would say that a whole is intrinsically good, whenever and only when it contains an excess of pleasure over pain; intrinsically bad, whenever and only when it contains an excess of pain over pleasure; and intrinsically indifferent, whenever and only when it contains neither.

In addition, therefore, to laying down precise rules as to what things are intrinsically *better* or *worse* than others, our theory also lays down equally precise ones as to what things are intrinsically *good* and *bad* and *indifferent*. By saying that a thing is intrinsically good it means that it would be a good thing that the thing in question should exist, even if it existed *quite alone,* without any further accompaniments or effects whatever. By saying that it is intrinsically bad, it means that it would be a bad thing or an evil that it should exist, even if it existed quite alone, without any further accompaniments or effects whatever. And by saying that it is intrinsically indifferent, it means that, if it existed *quite alone,* its existence would be neither a good nor an evil in any degree whatever. And just as the conceptions 'intrinsically better' and 'intrinsically worse' are connected in a perfectly precise manner with the conceptions 'right' and 'wrong', so, it maintains, are these other conceptions also. To say of anything, A, that it is 'intrinsically good', is equivalent to saying that, if we had to choose between an action of which A would be the sole or total effect, and an action, which would have absolutely no effects at all, it would always be our duty to choose the former, and wrong to choose the latter. And similarly to say of anything, A, that it is 'intrinsically bad', is equivalent to saying that, if we had to choose between an action of which A would be the sole effect, and an action which would have absolutely no effects at all, it would always be our duty to choose the latter and wrong to choose the former. And finally, to say of anything, A, that it is 'intrinsically indifferent', is equivalent to saying that, if we had to choose between an action, of which A would be the sole effect, and an action which would have absolutely no effects at all, it would not matter which we chose: either choice would be equally right.

To sum up, then, we may say that, in its second part, our theory lays down three principles. It asserts (1) that anything whatever, whether it be a single effect, or a whole set of effects, or a whole Universe, is *intrinsically good,* whenever and only when it either is or contains an excess of pleasure over pain; that anything whatever is *intrinsically bad,* whenever and only when it either is or contains an excess of pain over pleasure; and that all other things, no matter what their nature may be, are intrinsically indifferent. It asserts (2) that any one thing, whether it be a single effect, or a whole set of effects, or a whole Universe, is intrinsically *better* than another, whenever and only when the two are related to one another in one or other of the five following ways: namely, when either (*a*) while both are intrinsically good, the second is not so good as the first; or (*b*) while the first is intrinsically good, the second is intrinsically indifferent; or (*c*) while the first is intrinsically good, the second is intrinsically bad; or (*d*) while the first is intrinsically indifferent, the second is intrinsically bad; or (*e*) while both are intrinsically bad, the first is not so bad as the second. And it asserts (3) that, if we had to choose between two actions one of which would have intrinsically better total effects than the other, it always would be our duty to choose the former, and wrong to choose the latter; and that no action ever can be right *if* we could have done anything else instead which would have had intrinsically better total effects, nor wrong, *unless* we could have done something else instead which would have had intrinsically better total effects. From these three principles taken together, the whole theory follows. And whether it be true or false, it is, I think, at least a perfectly clear and intelligible theory. Whether it is or is not of any practical importance is, indeed, another question. But, even if it were of none whatever, it certainly lays down propositions of so fundamental and so far-reaching a character, that it seems worth while to consider whether they are true or false. There remain, I think, only two points which should be noticed with regard to it, before we go on to consider the principal objections which may be urged against it.

It should be noticed, first, that, though this theory asserts that nothing is *intrinsically* good, unless it is or contains an excess of pleasure over pain, it is very far from asserting that nothing is *good*, unless it fulfils this condition. By saying that a thing is *intrinsically good*, it means, as has been explained, that the existence of the thing in question *would* be a good, even if it existed quite alone, without any accompaniments or effects whatever; and it is quite plain that when we call things 'good' we by no means always mean this: we by no means always mean that they *would* be good, even if they existed quite alone. Very often, for instance, when we say that a thing is 'good', we mean that it is good *because of its effects*; and we should not for a moment maintain that it *would* be good, even if it had no effects at all. We are, for instance, familiar with the idea that it is sometimes a good thing for people to suffer pain; and yet we should be very loth to maintain that in all such cases their suffering *would* be a good thing, even if nothing were gained by it—if it had no further effects. We do, in general, maintain that suffering is good, only *where* and *because* it has further good effects. And similarly with many other things. Many things, therefore, which are *not* 'intrinsically' good, may nevertheless be 'good' in some one or other of the senses in which we use that highly ambiguous word. And hence our theory can and would quite consistently maintain that, while nothing is *intrinsically* good except pleasure or wholes which contain pleasure, many other things really are 'good'; and similarly that, while nothing is *intrinsically* bad except pain or wholes which contain it, yet many other things are really 'bad'. It would, for instance, maintain that it is *always* a good thing to act rightly, and a bad thing to act wrongly; although it would say at the same time that, since actions, strictly speaking, do not *contain* either pleasure or pain, but are only accompanied by or causes of them, a right action is *never intrinsically* good, nor a wrong one *intrinsically* bad. And similarly it would maintain that it is perfectly true that some men are 'good', and others 'bad', and some better than others; although no man can strictly be said to *contain* either pleasure or pain, and hence none can be either intrinsically good or intrinsically bad or intrinsically better than any other. It would even maintain (and this also it can do quite consistently), that events which are *intrinsically* good are nevertheless very often bad, and intrinsically bad ones good. It would, for instance, say that it is often a very bad thing for a man to enjoy a particular pleasure on a particular occasion, although the event, which consists in his enjoying it, may be intrinsically good, since it contains an excess of pleasure over pain. It may often be a very bad thing that such an event should happen, because it *causes* the man himself or other beings to have less pleasure or more pain in the future, than they would otherwise have had. And for similar reasons it may often be a very good thing that an intrinsically bad event should happen.

It is important to remember all this, because otherwise the theory may appear much more paradoxical than it really is. It may, for instance, appear, at first sight, as if it denied all value to anything except pleasure and wholes which contain it—a view which would be extremely paradoxical if it were held. But it does *not* do this. It does not deny all value to other things, but only all *intrinsic* value—a very different thing. It only says that none of them *would* have any value if they existed quite alone. But, of course, as a matter of fact, none of them do exist quite alone, and hence it may quite consistently allow that, as it is, many of them do have very great value. Concerning kinds of value, other than intrinsic value, it does not profess to lay down any general rules at all. And its reason for confining itself to intrinsic value is because it holds that this and this alone is related to right and wrong in the perfectly definite manner explained above. Whenever an action is right, it is right only if and because the total effects of no action, which the agent could have done instead, would have had more *intrinsic* value; and whenever an action is wrong, it is wrong only if and because the total effects of some other action, which the agent could have done instead, would have had more *intrinsic* value. This proposition, which is true of *intrinsic* value, is not, it holds, true of value of any other kind.

And a second point which should be noticed about this theory is the following. It is often represented as asserting that pleasure is the only thing which is *ultimately* good or desirable, and pain the only thing which is *ultimately* bad or undesirable; or as asserting that pleasure is the only thing which is good *for its own sake*, and pain the only thing which is bad *for its own sake*. And there is, I think, a sense in which it does assert this. But these expressions are not commonly carefully defined; and it is worth noticing that, if our theory does assert these propositions, the expressions *'ultimately* good' or 'good *for its own sake'* must be understood in a different sense from that which has been assigned above to the expression *'intrinsically* good'. We must not take *'ultimately* good' or 'good *for its own sake'* to be synonyms for *'intrinsically* good'. For our theory most emphatically does *not* assert that pleasure is the only thing *intrinsically* good, and pain the only thing *intrinsically* evil. On the contrary, it asserts that any whole which *contains* an excess of pleasure over pain is *intrinsically* good, no matter how much else it may contain besides; and similarly that any whole which contains an excess of pain over pleasure is *intrinsically* bad. This distinction between the conception expressed by *'ultimately* good' or 'good *for its own sake',* on the one hand, and that expressed by *'intrinsically* good', on the other, is not commonly made; and yet obviously we must make it, if we are to say that our theory does assert that pleasure is the only *ultimate* good, and pain the only *ultimate* evil. The two conceptions, if used in this way, have one important point in common, namely, that both of them will only apply to things whose existence *would* be good, even if they existed quite alone. Whether we assert that a thing is 'ultimately good' or 'good for its own sake' or 'intrinsically good', we are always asserting that it would be good, even if it existed quite alone. But the two conceptions differ in respect of the fact that, whereas a whole which is 'intrinsically good' may contain parts which are *not* intrinsically good, i.e. *would* not be good, if they existed quite alone; anything which is 'ultimately good' or 'good for its own sake' can contain no such parts. This, I think, is the meaning which we must assign to the expressions 'ultimately good' or 'good for its own sake', if we are to say that our theory asserts pleasure to be the *only* thing 'ultimately good' or 'good for its own sake'. We may, in short, divide intrinsically good things into two classes: namely (1) those which, while as wholes they are intrinsically good, nevertheless contain some parts which are not intrinsically good; and (2) those, which either have no parts at all, or, if they have any, have none but what are themselves intrinsically good. And we may thus, if we please, confine the terms 'ultimately good' or 'good for their own sakes' to things which belong to the second of these two classes. We may, of course, make a precisely similar distinction between two classes of intrinsically bad things. And it is only if we do this that our theory can be truly said to assert that nothing is 'ultimately good' or 'good for its own sake', except pleasure; and nothing 'ultimately bad' or 'bad for its own sake', except pain.

Such is the ethical theory which I have chosen to state, because it seems to me particularly simple, and hence to bring out particularly clearly some of the main questions which have formed the subject of ethical discussion.

What is specially important is to distinguish the question, which it professes to answer in its first part, from the much more radical questions, which it professes to answer in its second. In its first part, it only professes to answer the question: What characteristic is there which does actually, *as a matter of fact,* belong to all right voluntary actions, which ever have been or will be done in this world? While, in its second part, it professes to answer the much more fundamental question: What characteristic is there which *would* belong to absolutely any voluntary action, which was right, in any conceivable Universe, and under any conceivable circumstances? These two questions are obviously extremely different, and by the theory I have stated I mean a theory which does profess to give an answer to *both*.

Whether this theory has ever been held in exactly the form in which I have stated it, I should not like to say. But many people have certainly held something very like it; and it seems to be what is *often* meant by the familiar name 'Utilitarianism', which is the reason why I have chosen this name as the title of these two chapters. It must not, however, be assumed that anybody who talks about 'Utilitarianism' *always* means precisely this theory in all its details. On the contrary, many even of those who call themselves Utilitarians would object to some of its most fundamental propositions. One of the difficulties which occurs in ethical discussions is that no single name, which has ever been proposed as the name of an ethical theory, has any absolutely fixed significance. On the contrary, every name may be, and often is, used as a name for several different theories, which may differ from one another in very important respects. Hence, whenever anybody uses such a name, you can never trust to the name alone, but must always look carefully to see exactly what he means by it. For this reason I do not propose, in what follows, to give any name at all to this theory which I have stated, but will refer to it simply as the theory stated in these first two chapters.

III THE OBJECTIVITY OF MORAL JUDGEMENTS

Against the theory, which has been stated in the last two chapters, an enormous variety of different objections may be urged; and I cannot hope to deal with nearly all of them. What I want to do is to choose out those, which seem to me to be the most important, because they are the most apt to be strongly felt, and because they concern extremely general questions of principle. It seems to me that some of these objections are well founded, and that others are not, according as they are directed against different parts of what our theory asserts. And I propose, therefore, to split up the theory into parts, and to consider separately the chief objections which might be urged against each of these different parts.

And we may begin with an extremely fundamental point. Our theory plainly implied two things. It implied (1) that, if it is true at any one time that a particular voluntary action is right, it must *always* be true of that particular action that it *was* right: or, in other words, that an action cannot change from right to wrong, or from wrong to right; that it cannot possibly be true of the very same action that it is right at one time and wrong at another. And it implied also (2) that the same action cannot possibly *at the same time* be both right and wrong. It plainly implied both these two things because it asserted that a voluntary action can only be right, if it produces a maximum of pleasure, and can only be wrong, if it produces less than a maximum. And obviously, if it is *once* true of any action that it did produce a maximum of pleasure, it must *always* be true of it that it did; and obviously also it cannot be true at one and the same time of one and the same action both that it did produce a maximum of pleasure and also that it produced less than a maximum. Our theory implied, therefore, that any particular action cannot possibly be *both* right and wrong either at the same time or at different times. At any particular time it must be either right or wrong, and, whichever it is at any one time, it will be the same at all times.

It must be carefully noticed, however, that our theory only implies that this is true of any *particular* voluntary action, which we may choose to consider: it does not imply that the same is ever true of a *class* of actions. That is to say, it implies that *if*, at the time when Brutus murdered Caesar, this action of his was right, then, it must be equally true now, and will always be true, that this particular action of Brutus was right, and it never can have been and never will be true that it was *wrong*. Brutus' action on this particular occasion cannot, it says, have been both right and wrong; and if it was once true that it was right, then it must always be true that it was right; or if it was once true that it was wrong, it must always be true that it was wrong. And similarly with every other absolutely particular action, which actually was done or might have been done by a particular man on a particular occasion. Of every such action, our theory says, it is true that it cannot at any time have been both right and wrong; and also that, whichever of these two predicates it possessed at any one time, it must possess the same at all times. But it does *not* imply that the same is true of any particular *class* of actions—of murder, for instance. It does not assert that if one murder, committed at one time, was wrong, then any other murder committed at the same time must also have been wrong; nor that if one murder, committed at one time, is wrong, any other murder committed at any other time must be wrong. On the contrary, though it does not directly imply that this is false, yet it does imply that it is unlikely that any particular *class* of actions will absolutely always be right or absolutely always wrong. For, it holds, as we have seen, that the question whether an action is right or wrong depends upon its effects; and the question what effects an action will produce depends, of course, not only upon the *class* to which it belongs, but also on the particular circumstances in which it is done. While, in one set of circumstances, a particular kind of action may produce good effects, in other circumstances a precisely similar action may produce bad ones. And, since the circumstances are always changing, it is extremely unlikely (though not impossible) that actions of any particular class, such as murder or adultery, should absolutely *always* be right or absolutely *always* wrong. Our theory, therefore, does not imply that, if an action *of a particular class* is right once, every other action *of the same class* must always be right: on the contrary, it follows from its view that this is unlikely to be true. What it does imply, is that if we consider any particular *instance* of any class, that particular *instance* cannot ever be both right and wrong, and if once right, must always be right. And it is extremely important to distinguish clearly between these two different questions, because they are liable to be confused. When we ask whether *the same* action can be both right and wrong we may mean two entirely different things by this question. We may merely mean to ask: Can the same *kind* of action be right at one time and wrong at another, or right and wrong simultaneously? And to this question our theory would be inclined to answer: It can. Or else by *the same* action, we may mean not merely the same *kind* of action, but some single absolutely particular action, which was or might have been performed by a definite person on a definite occasion. And it is to *this* question that our theory replies: It is absolutely impossible that any one single, absolutely particular action can ever be both right and wrong, either at the same time or at different times.

Now this question as to whether one and the same action can ever be both right and wrong at the same time, or can ever be right at one time and wrong at another, is, I think, obviously, an extremely fundamental one. If we decide it in the affirmative, then a great many of the questions which have been most discussed by ethical writers are at once put out of court. It must, for instance, be idle to discuss what characteristic there is, which universally distinguishes right actions from wrong ones, if this view be true. If one and the same action can be both right and wrong, then obviously there can be *no* such characteristic—there can be no characteristic which *always* belongs to right actions, and *never* to wrong ones: since, if so much as one single action is *both* right and wrong, this action must possess any characteristic (if there is one) which *always* belongs to right actions, and, at the same time, since the action is also wrong, this characteristic cannot be one which *never* belongs to wrong actions. Before, therefore, we enter on any discussions as to what characteristic there is which *always* belongs to right actions and *never* to wrong ones, it is extremely important that we should satisfy ourselves, if we can, that one and the same action cannot be both right and wrong, either at the same time or at different times. For, if this is not the case, then all such discussions must be absolutely futile. I propose, therefore, first of all, to raise the simple issue: Can one and the same action be both right and wrong, either at the time or at different times? Is the theory stated in the last two chapters in the right, so far as it merely asserts that this cannot be the case?

Now I think that most of those who hold, as this theory does, that one and the same action cannot be both right and wrong, simply assume that this is the case, without trying to prove it. It is, indeed, quite common to find the mere fact that a theory implies the contrary, used as a conclusive argument against that theory. It is argued: Since this theory implies that one and the same action can be both right and wrong, and since it is evident that this cannot be so, therefore the theory in question must be false. And, for my part, it seems to me that such a method of argument is perfectly justified. It does seem to me to be evident that no voluntary action can be both right and wrong; and I do not see how this can be proved by reference to any principle which is more certain than it is itself. If, therefore, anybody asserts that the contrary is evident to him—that it is evident to him that one and the same action *can* be both right and wrong, I do not see how it can be *proved* that he is wrong. If the question is reduced to these ultimate terms, it must, I think, simply be left to the reader's inspection. Like all ultimate questions, it is incapable of strict proof either way. But most of those who hold that an action can be both right and wrong are, I think, in fact influenced by certain considerations, which do admit of argument. They hold certain views, from which this conclusion follows; and it is only because they hold these views that they adopt the conclusion. There are, I think, two views, in particular, which are very commonly held and which are specially influential in leading people to adopt it. And it is very important that we should consider these two views carefully, both because they lead to this conclusion and for other reasons.

The first of them is as follows. It may be held, namely, that, whenever we assert that an action or class of actions is right or wrong, we must be merely making an assertion about somebody's *feelings* towards the action or class of actions in question. This is a view which seems to be very commonly held in some form or other; and one chief reason why it is held is, I think, that many people seem to find an extreme difficulty in seeing what else we possibly *can* mean by the words 'right' and 'wrong', except that some mind or set of minds has some feeling, or some other mental attitude, towards the actions

to which we apply these predicates. In some of its forms this view does
not lead to the consequence that one and the same action may be both
right and wrong; and with these forms we are not concerned just at
present. But some of the forms in which it may be held do directly lead
to this consequence; and where people do hold that one and the same
action may be both right and wrong, it is, I think, very generally because they hold this view in one of these forms. There are several different forms of it which do lead to this consequence, and they are apt,
I think, not to be clearly distinguished from one another. People are
apt to assume that in our judgements of right and wrong we must be
making an assertion about the feelings of *some* man or *some* group of
men, without trying definitely to make up their minds as to who the
man or group of men can be about whose feelings we are making it. So
soon as this question is fairly faced, it becames plain, I think, that
there are serious objections to any possible alternative.

To begin with, it may be held that whenever any man asserts an
action to be right or wrong, what he is asserting is merely that he
himself has some particular feeling towards the action in question.
Each of us, according to this view, is merely making an assertion
about *his own* feelings: when *I* assert that an action is right, the
whole of what I mean is merely that *I* have some particular feeling
towards the action; and when *you* make the same assertion, the *whole*
of what you mean is merely that *you* have the feeling in question
towards the action. Different views may, of course, be taken as to
what the feeling is which we are supposed to assert that we have.
Some people might say that, when we call an action right, we are
merely asserting that we *like* it or are *pleased* with it; and that when
we call one wrong, we are merely asserting that we *dislike* it or are
displeased with it. Others might say, more plausibly, that it is not
mere liking and dislike that we express by these judgements, but a
peculiar sort of liking and dislike, which might perhaps be called a
feeling of *moral approval* and of *moral disapproval*. Others, again,
might, perhaps, say that it is not a pair of opposite feelings which are
involved, but merely the presence or absence of one particular feeling: that, for instance, when we call an action wrong, we merely
mean to say that we have towards it a feeling of disapproval, and that
by calling it right, we mean to say, not that we have towards it a
positive feeling of approval, but merely that we have *not* got towards
it the feeling of disapproval. But whatever view be taken as to the
precise nature of the feelings about which we are supposed to be

making a judgement, *any* view which holds that, when we call an action right or wrong, each of us is always merely asserting that he *himself* has or has not some particular feeling towards it, does, I think, inevitably lead to the same conclusion—namely, that quite often one and the same action is *both* right and wrong; and *any* such view is also exposed to one and the same fatal objection.

The argument which shows that such views inevitably lead to the conclusion that one and the same action is quite often both right and wrong, consists of two steps, each of which deserves to be separately emphasized.

The first is this. If, whenever I judge an action to be right, I am merely judging that I myself have a particular feeling towards it, then it plainly follows that, provided I really have the feeling in question, my judgement is true, and therefore the action in question really is right. And what is true of me, in this respect, will also be true of any other man. No matter what we suppose the feeling to be, it must be true that, whenever and so long as *any* man really has towards any action the feeling in question, then, and for just so long, the action in question really is right. For what our theory supposes is that, when a man judges an action to be right, he is merely judging *that* he has this feeling towards it; and hence, whenever he really has it, his judgement must be true, and the action really must be right. It strictly follows, therefore, from this theory that whenever *any man whatever* really has a particular feeling towards an action, the action really is right; and whenever *any man whatever* really has another particular feeling towards an action, the action really is wrong. Or, if we take the view that it is not a pair of feelings which are in question, but merely the presence or absence of a single feeling—for instance, the feeling of moral disapproval; then, what follows is, that whenever any man whatever fails to have this feeling towards an action, the action really is right, and whenever any man whatever has got the feeling, the action really is wrong. Whatever view we take as to what the feelings are, and whether we suppose that it is a pair of feelings or merely the presence and absence of a single one, the consequence follows that the presence (or absence) of the feeling in question in *any man whatever* is sufficient to ensure that an action is right or wrong, as the case may be. And it is important to insist that this consequence does follow, because it is not, I think, always clearly seen. It seems sometimes to be vaguely held that when a man judges an action to be right, he is merely judging that he has a particular feeling towards it, but that yet, though he really has this feeling, the action is not necessarily really right. But obviously this is impossible. If the *whole* of what we mean to assert, when we say that an action is right, is merely that we have a particular feeling towards it, then plainly, provided only we really have this feeling, the action *must* really be right.

It follows, therefore, from any view of this type, that, whenever *any* man has (or has not) some particular feeling towards an action, the action is right; and also that, whenever *any* man has (or has not) some particular feeling towards an action, the action is wrong. And now, if we take into account a second fact, it seems plainly to follow that, if this be so, one and the same action must quite often be both right and wrong.

This second fact is merely the observed fact, which it seems difficult to deny, that, whatever pair of feelings or single feeling we take, cases do occur in which two different men have opposite feelings towards the same action, and in which, while one has a given feeling towards an action, the other has not got it. It might, perhaps, be thought that it is possible to find *some* pair of feelings or *some* single feeling, in the case of which this rule does not hold: that, for instance, no man ever *really* feels moral approval towards an action, towards which another feels moral disapproval. This is a view which people are apt to take, because, where we have a strong feeling of moral disapproval towards an action, we may find it very difficult to believe that any other man *really* has a feeling of moral approval towards the same action, or even that he regards it without some degree of moral disapproval. And there is some excuse for this view in the fact, that when a man says that an action is right, and even though he sincerely believes it to be so, it may nevertheless be the case that he really *feels* towards it some degree of moral disapproval. That is to say, though it is certain that men's *opinions* as to what is right and wrong often differ, it is not certain that their *feelings* always differ when their opinions do. But still, if we look at the extraordinary differences that there have been and are between different races of mankind, and in different stages of society, in respect of the classes of actions which have been regarded as right and wrong, it is, I think, scarcely possible to doubt that, in some societies, actions have been regarded with actual *feelings* of positive moral approval, towards which many of us would feel the strongest disapproval. And if this is so with regard to *classes* of actions, it can hardly fail to be sometimes the case with regard to *particular* actions. We may, for instance, read of a particular action, which excites in us a strong feeling of moral disapproval; and yet it can hardly be doubted that sometimes this very action will have been regarded by some of the men among whom it was done, without any feeling of disapproval whatever, and even with a feeling of positive approval. But, if this be so, then, on the view we are considering, it will absolutely follow that whereas it was true *then,* when it was done, that that action was right, it is true *now* that the very same action was wrong.

And once we admit that there have been such real differences of feeling between men in different stages of society, we must also, I think, admit that such differences do quite often exist even among contemporaries, when they are members of very different societies; so that one and the same action may quite often be *at the same time* both right and wrong. And, having admitted this, we ought, I think, to go still further. Once we are convinced that real differences of *feeling* towards certain classes of actions, and not merely differences of opinion, do exist between men in different states of society, the probability is that when two men in the same state of society differ in opinion as to whether an action is right or wrong, this difference of opinion, though it by no means always indicates a corresponding difference of feeling, yet sometimes really is accompanied by such a difference: so that two members of the *same* society may really sometimes have opposite feelings towards one and the same action, *whatever feeling we take.* And finally, we must admit, I think, that even one and the same individual may experience such a change of feeling towards one and the same action. A man certainly does often come to change his *opinion* as to whether a particular action was right or wrong; and we must, I think, admit that, sometimes at least, his feelings towards it completely change as well; so that, for instance, an action, which he formerly regarded with moral disapproval, he may now regard with positive moral approval, and *vice versa.* So that, for this reason alone, and quite apart from differences of feeling between different men, we shall have to admit, according to our theory, that it is often *now* true of an action that it *was* right, although it was formerly true of the same action that it *was* wrong.

This fact, on which I have been insisting, that different men do feel differently towards the same action, and that even the same man may feel differently towards it at different times, is, of course, a mere commonplace; and my only excuse for insisting on it is that it might possibly be thought that some one feeling or pair of feelings, and those the very ones which it is most plausible to regard as *the* ones about which we are making an assertion in our judgements of right and wrong, are exceptions to the rule. I think, however, we must recognize that no feeling or pair of feelings, which could possibly be maintained to be *the* ones with which our judgements of right and wrong are concerned, does, in fact, form an exception. Whatever feeling you take, it seems hardly possible to doubt that instances have actually occurred, in which, while one man really had the feeling in question towards a given action, other men have *not* had it, and some of them have even had an opposite one, towards the same action. There may, perhaps, be *some* classes of actions in the case of which this has never occurred; but what seems certain is that there are *some* classes, with which it has occurred: and, if there are any *at all*, that is sufficient to establish our conclusion. For if this is so, and if, when a man asserts an action to be right or wrong, he is always merely asserting that he himself has some particular feeling towards it, then it absolutely follows that one and the same action has sometimes been *both* right and wrong—right at one time and wrong at another, or both simultaneously.

And I think that some argument of this sort is the chief reason why many people are apt to hold that one and the same action may be both right and wrong. They are much impressed by the fact that different men do feel quite differently towards the same classes of action, and, holding also that, when we judge an action to be right or wrong, we *must* be merely making a judgement about somebody's feelings, it seems impossible to avoid the conclusion that one and the same action often *is* both right and wrong. This conclusion does not, indeed, necessarily follow from these two doctrines taken together. Whether it follows or not, depends on the precise form in which we hold the latter doctrine—upon *who* the somebody is about whose feelings we are making the assertion. But it *does* follow from the precise form of this doctrine which we are now considering—the form which asserts that each man is merely making an assertion about *his own* feelings. And, since this is one of the most plausible forms in which the doctrine can be held, it is extremely important to consider, whether it can be true in this form. Can it possibly be the case, then, that, when we judge an action to be right or wrong, each of us is only asserting that *he himself* has some particular feeling towards it?

It seems to me that there is an absolutely fatal objection to the view that this is the case. It must be remembered that the question is merely a question of fact; a question as to the actual analysis of our moral judgements—as to what it is that actually happens, when we *think* an action to be right or wrong. And if we remember that it is thus merely a question as to what we *actually* think, when we think an action to be right or wrong,—neither more nor less than this,—it can, I think, be clearly seen that the view we are considering is inconsistent with plain facts. This is so, because it involves a curious consequence, which those who hold it do not always seem to realize that it involves; and this consequence is, I think, plainly not in accordance with the facts. The consequence is this. If, when one man says, 'This action is right', and another answers, 'No, it is not right', each of them is always merely making an assertion about *his own* feelings, it plainly follows that there is never really any difference of opinion between them: the one of them is never really contradicting what the other is asserting. They are no more contradicting one another than if, when one had said, 'I like sugar', the other had answered, '*I don't* like sugar'. In such a case, there is, of course, no conflict of opinion, no contradiction of one by the other: for it may perfectly well be the case that what each asserts is equally true; it may quite well be the case that the one man really does like sugar, and the other really does *not* like it. The one, therefore, is *never* denying what the other is asserting. And what the view we are considering involves is that when one man holds an action to be right, and another holds it to be wrong or not right, here also the one is *never* denying what the other is asserting. It involves, therefore, the very curious consequence that no two men can ever differ in opinion as to whether an action is right or wrong. And surely the fact that it involves this consequence is sufficient to condemn it. It is surely plain matter of fact that when I assert an action to be wrong, and another man asserts it to be right, there sometimes is a real difference of opinion between us: he sometimes is denying the very thing which I am asserting. But, if this is so, then it cannot possibly be the case that each of us is merely making a judgement about his own feelings; since two such judgements never can contradict one another. We can, therefore, reduce the question whether this theory is true or not, to a very simple question of fact. Is it ever the case that when one man thinks that an action is right and another thinks it is *not* right, that the second really is thinking that the action has *not* got some predicate which the first thinks that it has got? I think, if we look at this question fairly, we must admit that it sometimes is the case; that both men may use the word 'right' to denote *exactly the same* predicate, and that the one may really be thinking that the action in question really has this predicate, while the other is thinking that it has *not* got it. But if this is so, then the theory we are considering certainly is not true. It cannot be true that every man always denotes by the word 'right' merely a relation to *his own* feelings, since, if that were so, no two men would ever denote by this word *the same* predicate; and hence a man who said that an action was *not* right could never be denying that it had the very predicate, which another, who said that it *was* right, was asserting that it had.

It seems to me this argument proves conclusively that, whatever we do mean, when we say that an action is right, we certainly do not mean merely that we *ourselves* have a certain feeling towards it. But it is important to distinguish carefully between exactly what it *does* prove, and what it does *not* prove. It does *not* prove, at all, that it may not be the case, that, whenever any man judges an action to be right, he always, in fact, *has* a certain feeling towards it, and even that he makes the judgement only *because* he has that feeling. It only proves that, even if this be so, *what* he is judging is not merely *that* he has the feeling. And these two points are, I think, very liable to be confused. It may be alleged to be a fact that whenever a man judges an action to be right, he only does so, *because* he has a certain feeling towards it; and this alleged fact actually be used as an argument to prove that *what* he is judging is merely *that* he has the feeling. But obviously, even if the alleged fact be a fact, it does not in the least support this conclusion. The two points are entirely different, and there is a most important difference between their consequences. The difference is that, even if it be true that a man never judges an action to be right, unless he has a certain feeling towards it, yet, if this be all, the mere fact that he has this feeling, will not prove his judgement to be true; we may quite well hold that, even though he has the feeling and judges the action to be right, yet sometimes his judgement is false and the action is not really right. But if, on the other hand, we hold that *what* he is judging is merely *that* he has the feeling, then the mere fact that he has it *will* prove his judgement to be true: if he is only judging *that* he has it, then the mere fact *that* he has it is, of course, sufficient to make his judgement true. We must, therefore, distinguish carefully between the assertion that, whenever a man judges an action to be right, he only does so *because* he has a certain feeling, and the entirely different assertion that, whenever he judges an action to be right, he is merely judging *that* he has this feeling. The former assertion, even if it be true, does not prove that the latter is true also. And we may, therefore, dispute the latter without disputing the former. It is *only* the latter which our argument proves to be untrue; and not a word has been said tending to show that the former may not be perfectly true.

Our argument, therefore, does not disprove the assertion, if it should be made, that we only judge actions to be right and wrong, *when* and *because* we have certain feelings towards them. And it is also important to insist that it does not disprove another assertion also. It does not disprove the assertion that, whenever any man has a certain feeling towards an action, the action is, *as a matter of fact,* always right. Anybody is still perfectly free to hold that this is true, *as a matter of fact,* and that, therefore, *as a matter of fact,* one and the same action often is both right and wrong, even if he admits what our argument does prove; namely, that, when a man *thinks* an action to be right or wrong, he is not merely *thinking* that he has some feeling towards it. The only importance of our argument, in this connexion, is merely that it destroys one of the main reasons for holding that this *is* true, as a matter of fact. If we once clearly see that to say that an action is right is not the same thing as to say that we have any feeling towards it, what reason is there left for holding that the presence of a certain feeling is, in fact, always a sign that it is right? No one, I think, would be very much tempted to assert that the mere presence (or absence) of a certain feeling is invariably a sign of rightness, but for the supposition that, in some way or other, the only possible meaning of the word 'right', as applied to actions, is that somebody has a certain feeling towards them. And it is this supposition, in one of its forms, that our argument does disprove.

But even if it be admitted that, in this precise form, the view is quite untenable, it may still be urged that nevertheless it is true in some other form, from which the same consequence will follow—namely, the consequence that one and the same action is quite often both right and wrong. Many people have such a strong disposition to believe that when we judge an action to be right or wrong we *must* be merely making an assertion about the feelings of *some* man or set of men, that, even if they are convinced that we are not always merely making an assertion, each about *his own* feelings, they will still be disposed to think that we must be making one about *somebody else's*. The difficulty is to find any man or set of men about whose feelings it can be plausibly held that we are making an assertion, if we are not merely making one about our own; but still there are two alternatives, which may seem, at first sight, to be just possible, namely (1) that each man, when he asserts an action to be right or wrong, is merely asserting that a certain feeling is *generally* felt towards actions of that class by most of the members of the society to which he belongs, or (2) merely that *some man or other* has a certain feeling towards them.

From either of these two views, it will, of course, follow that one and the same action is often both right and wrong, for the same reasons as were given in the last case. Thus, if, when *I* assert an action to be right, I am merely asserting that it is generally approved in the society to which *I* belong, it follows, of course, that if it *is* generally approved by my society, my assertion is true, and the action really *is* right. But as we saw, it seems undeniable, that some actions which are generally approved in *my* society, will have been disapproved or will still be disapproved in other societies. And, since any member of one of those societies will, on this view, when he judges an action to be wrong, be merely judging that it is disapproved in *his* society, it follows that when he judges one of these actions, which really is disapproved in his society, though approved in mine, to be *wrong*, this judgement of his will be just as true as *my* judgement that the same action was right: and hence the same action really will be both right and wrong. And similarly, if we adopt the other alternative, and say that when a man judges an action to be right he is merely judging that *some man or other* has a particular feeling towards it, it will, of course, follow that whenever any man at all really has this feeling towards it, the action really is right, while, whenever any man at all has *not* got it or has an opposite feeling, the action really is wrong: and, since cases will certainly occur in which one man has the required feeling, while another has an opposite one towards the same action, in all such cases the same action will be both right and wrong.

From either of these two views, then, the same consequence will follow. And, though I do not know whether any one would definitely hold either of them to be true, it is, I think, worth while briefly to consider the objections to them, because they seem to be the only alternatives left, from which this consequence will follow, when once we have rejected the view that, in our judgements of right and wrong, each of us is merely talking about *his own* feelings; and because, while the objection which did apply to that view, does not apply equally to these, there is an objection which does apply to these, but which does not apply nearly so obviously to that one.

The objection which was urged against that view does, indeed, apply, in a limited extent, to the first of these two: since if when a man judges an action to be right or wrong, he is always merely making an assertion about the feelings of *his own* society, it will follow that two men, who belong to *different* societies, can never possibly differ in opinion as to whether an action is right or wrong. But this objection does not apply as between two men who both belong to the *same* society. The view that when any man asserts an action to be right he is merely making an assertion about the feelings of *his own* society, does allow that two men belonging to the *same* society may really differ in opinion as to whether an action is right or wrong. Neither this view, therefore, nor the view that we are merely asserting that *some man or other* has a particular feeling towards the action in question involves the absurdity that *no* two men can ever differ in opinion as to whether an action is right or wrong. We cannot, therefore, urge the fact that they involve this absurdity as an objection against them, as we could against the view that each man is merely talking of *his own* feelings.

But both of them are nevertheless exposed to another objection, equally fatal, to which that view was not so obviously exposed. The objection is again merely one of psychological fact, resting upon observation of what actually happens when a man thinks an action to be right or wrong. For, whatever feeling or feelings we take as the ones about which he is supposed to be judging, it is quite certain that a man may think an action to be right, even when he does *not* think that the members of his society have in general the required feeling (or absence of feeling) towards it; and that similarly he may doubt whether an action is right, even when he does *not* doubt that *some man or other* has the required feeling towards it. Cases of this kind certainly constantly occur, and what they prove is that, whatever a man is thinking when he thinks an action to be right, he is certainly *not* merely thinking that his society has in general a particular feeling towards it; and similarly that, when he is in doubt as to whether an action is right, the question about which he is in doubt is not merely as to whether any man at all has the required feeling towards it. Facts of this kind are, therefore, absolutely fatal to both of these two theories; whereas in the case of the theory that he is merely making a judgement about *his own feelings,* it is not so obvious that there are any facts of the same kind inconsistent with it. For here it might be urged with some plausibility (though, I think, untruly) that when a man judges an action to be right he always does think that he himself has some particular feeling towards it; and similarly that when he is in doubt as to whether an action is right he always is in doubt as to his own feelings. But it cannot possibly be urged, with any plausibility at all, that when a man judges an action to be right he always thinks, for instance, that it is generally approved in his society; or that when he is in doubt, he is always in doubt as to whether *any* man approves it. He may know quite well that *somebody* does approve it, and yet be in doubt whether it is right; and he may be quite certain that his society does *not* approve it, and yet still think that it *is* right. And the same will hold, *whatever* feeling we take instead of moral approval.

These facts, then, seem to me to prove conclusively that, when a man judges an action to be right or wrong, he is *not* always merely judging that his society has some particular feeling towards actions of that class, nor yet that *some* man has. But here again it is important to insist on the limitations of the argument; and to distinguish clearly between what it *does* prove and what it does *not.* It does not, of course, prove that any class of action towards which any society has a particular feeling, may not, *as a matter of fact,* always be right; nor even that any action, towards which any man *whatever* has the feeling, may not, *as a matter of fact,* always be so. Anybody, while fully admitting the force of our argument, is still perfectly free to hold that these things are true, *as a matter of fact;* and hence that one and the same action often is both right and wrong. All that our arguments, taken together, do strictly prove, is that, when a man asserts an action to be right or wrong, he is *not* merely making an assertion either about his own feelings nor yet about those of the society in which he lives, nor yet merely that some man or other has some feeling towards it. This, and nothing more, is what they *prove.* But if we once admit that this much *is* proved, what reason have we left for asserting that it *is* true, *as a matter of fact,* that whatever any society or any man has a particular feeling towards, always is right? It *may*, of course, be true as a matter of fact; but is there any reason for supposing that it is? If the predicate which we mean by the word 'right', and which, therefore, must belong to every action which really is right, is something quite different from a mere relation to anybody's feelings, why should we suppose that such a relation does, in fact, always go along with it; and that this predicate always belongs, *in addition*, to every action which has the required relation to somebody's feelings? If rightness is not the same thing as the having a relation to the feelings of any man or set of men, it would be a curious coincidence, if any such relation were invariably a sign of rightness. What we have proved is that rightness is *not* the same thing as any such relation; and if that be so, then, the probability is that even where an action has the required relation to somebody's feelings, it will *not* always be right.

There are, then, conclusive reasons against the view that, when we assert an action to be right or wrong, we are merely asserting that somebody has a particular feeling towards it, in any of the forms in which it will follow from this view that one and the same action can be both right and wrong. And we can, I think, also see that one of the reasons, which seems to have had most influence in leading people to suppose that this view *must* be true, in some form or other, is quite without weight. The reason I mean is one drawn from certain considerations as to the *origin* of our moral judgements. It has been widely held that, in the history of the human race, judgements of right and wrong *originated* in the fact that primitive men or their non-human ancestors had certain feelings towards certain classes of actions. That is to say, it is supposed that there was a time, if we go far enough back, when our ancestors *did* have different feelings towards different actions, being, for instance, pleased with some and displeased with others, but when they did *not*, as yet, judge any actions to be right or wrong; and that it was only because they transmitted these feelings, more or less modified, to their descendants, that those descendants at some later stage, began to make judgements of right and wrong; so that, in a sense, our moral judgements were *developed out of* mere feelings. And I can see no objection to the supposition that this was so. But, then, it seems also to be often supposed that, if our moral judgements were developed out of feelings—if this was their origin—they must *still* at this moment be somehow concerned with feelings: that the developed product must resemble the germ out of which it was developed in this particular respect. And this is an assumption for which there is, surely, no shadow of ground. It is admitted, on all hands, that the developed product does always differ, in some respects, from its origin; and the precise respects in which it differs is a matter which can only be settled by observation: we cannot lay down a universal rule that it *must* always resemble it in certain definite respects. Thus, even those who hold that our moral judgements are merely judgements about feelings must admit that, at some point in the history of the human race, men, or their ancestors, began not merely to *have* feelings but to *judge* that they had them: and this alone means an enormous change. If such a change as this must have occurred at some time or other, without our being able to say precisely when or why, what reason is there, why another change, which is scarcely greater, should not also have occurred, either before or after it? a change consisting in the fact that men for the first time become conscious of another predicate, which might attach to actions, beside the mere fact that certain feelings were felt towards them, and began to judge of this other predicate that it did or did not belong to certain actions? It is certain that, if men have been developed from non-human ancestors at all, there must have been many occasions on which they became possessed for the first time of some new idea. And why should not the ideas, which we convey by the words 'right' and 'wrong', be among the number, even if these ideas do *not* merely consist in the thought that some man has a particular feeling towards some action? There is no more reason why such an idea should not have been developed out of the mere existence of a feeling than why the judgement that we *have* feelings should not have been developed from the same origin. And hence the theory that moral judgements originated in feelings does not, in fact, lend any support at all to the theory that now, as developed, they can only be judgements *about* feelings. No argument from the origin of a thing can be a safe guide as to exactly what the nature of the thing is now. That is a question which must be settled by actual analysis of the thing in its present state. And such analysis seems plainly to show that moral judgements are *not* merely judgements about feelings.

I conclude, then, that the theory that our judgements of right and wrong are merely judgements about somebody's feelings is quite un-tenable in any of the forms in which it will lead to the conclusion that one and the same action is often both right and wrong. But I said that this was only one out of two theories, which seem to be those which have the most influence in leading people to adopt this conclusion. And we must now briefly consider the second of these two theories.

This second theory is one which is often confused with the one just considered. It consists in asserting that when we judge an action to be right or wrong what we are asserting is merely that somebody or other *thinks* it to be right or wrong. That is to say, just as the last theory asserted that our moral judgements are merely judgements about somebody's *feelings*, this one asserts that they are merely judgements about somebody's *thoughts* or opinions. And they are apt to be confused with one another because a man's *feelings* with regard to an action are not always clearly distinguished from his *opinion* as to whether it is right or wrong. Thus one and the same word is often used, sometimes to express the fact that a man has a *feeling* towards an action, and sometimes to express the fact that he has an *opinion* about it. When, for instance, we say that a man *approves* an action, we may mean *either* that he has a feeling towards it, *or* that he *thinks* it to be right; and so too, when we say that he *disapproves* it, we may mean *either* that he has a certain feeling towards it, *or* that he thinks it to be wrong. But yet it is quite plain that to have a feeling towards an action, no matter what feeling we take, is a different thing from judging it to be right or wrong. Even if we were to adopt one of the views just rejected and to say that to judge an action to be right or wrong is the same thing as to judge that we have a feeling towards it, it would still follow that to make the judgement is something different from merely *having* the feeling; for a man may certainly *have* a feeling, without thinking that he has it; or think that he has it, without having it. We must, therefore, distinguish between the theory that to say that an action is right or wrong is the same thing as to say that somebody has some kind of *feeling* towards it, and the theory that it is the same thing as to say that somebody *thinks* it to be right or wrong.

This latter theory, however, may be held in the same three different forms, as the former; and in whichever form it is held, it will lead to the same conclusion—namely, that one and the same action is very often both right and wrong—and for the same reasons. If, for instance, when I say that an action is right, all that I mean is that I *think* it to be right, it will follow, that, if I do really think it to be right, my judgement *that* I think so will be true; and since this judgement is supposed to be identical with the judgement that it *is* right, it will follow that the judgement that it is right is true and hence that the action really is right. And since it is even more obvious that different men's opinions as to whether a given action is right or wrong differ both at the same time and at different times, than that their feelings towards the same action differ, it will follow that one and the same action very often *is* both right and wrong. And just as the conclusion which follows from this theory is the same as that which followed from the last, so also, in each of the three different forms in which it may be held, it is open to exactly the same objections. Thus, in its first form, it will involve the absurdity that no two men ever differ in opinion as to whether an action is right or wrong, and will thus contradict a plain fact. While in the other two forms, it will involve the conclusions that no man ever thinks an action to be right, unless he thinks that his society thinks it to be right, and that no man ever doubts whether an action is right, unless he doubts whether any man at all thinks it right—two conclusions which are both of them certainly untrue.

These objections are, I think, sufficient by themselves to dispose of this theory as of the last; but it is worth while to dwell on it a little longer, because it is also exposed to another objection, of quite a different order, to which the last was not exposed, and because it owes its plausibility partly, I think, to the fact that it is liable to be confused with another theory, which may be expressed in exactly the same words, and which may quite possibly be true.

The special objection to which this theory is exposed consists in the fact that it is in all cases totally impossible that, when we believe a given thing, *what* we believe should merely be that we (or anybody else) have the belief in question. This is impossible, because, if it were the case, we should not be believing anything at all. For let us suppose it to be the case: let us suppose that, when I believe that A is B, what I am believing is merely *that* somebody believes that A is B. What I am believing, on this supposition, is merely that somebody (either myself or somebody else) entertains the belief that A is B. But what *is* this belief which I am believing that somebody entertains? According to the theory it is itself, in its turn, merely the belief *that somebody believes* that A is B. So that what I am believing turns out to be that somebody believes *that somebody believes*—that A is B. But here again, we may substitute for the phrase 'that A is B', what is supposed to be identical with it—namely, *that somebody believes,* that A is B. And here again we may make the same substitution; and so on absolutely *ad infinitum.* So that what I am believing will turn out to be that somebody believes, that somebody believes, that somebody believes, that somebody believes . . . *ad infinitum.* Always, when I try to state, *what* it is that the somebody believes, I shall find it to be again merely *that* somebody believes . . . , and I shall never get to anything whatever which is *what* is believed. But thus to believe that somebody believes, that somebody believes, that somebody believes . . . quite indefinitely, without *ever* coming to anything which is what is believed, is to believe nothing at all. So that, if this were the case, there could be no such belief as the belief that A is B. We must, therefore, admit that, in no case whatever, when we believe a given thing, can the given thing in question be merely *that* we ourselves (or somebody else) believe the very same given thing. And since this is true in all cases, it must be true in our special case. It is totally impossible, therefore, that to believe an action to be right can be the same thing as believing that we ourselves or somebody else believe it to be right.

But the fact that this view is untenable is, I think, liable to be obscured by the fact that we often express, in the same words, another view, quite different from this, which may quite well be true. When a man asserts that an action is right or wrong, it may quite well be true, in a sense, that all that he is *expressing* by this assertion is the fact that he *thinks* it to be right or wrong. The truth is that there is an important distinction, which is not always observed, between what a man *means* by a given assertion and what he *expresses* by it. Whenever we make any assertion whatever (unless we do not mean what we say) we are always *expressing* one or other of two things—namely, either that we *think* the thing in question to be so or that we *know* it to be so. If, for instance, I say 'A is B', and mean what I say, what I *mean* is always merely that A *is* B; but those words of mine will always also *express* either the fact that *I think* that A is B, or the fact that *I know* it to be so; and even where I do not mean what I say, my words may be said to *imply* either that I think that A is B or that I know it, since they will commonly lead people to suppose that one or other of these two things is the case. Whenever, therefore, a man asserts that an action is right or wrong, what he *expresses* or *implies* by these words will be either that he thinks it to be so or that he knows it to be so, although neither of these two things can possibly constitute the whole of what he *means* to assert.

And it is quite possible to hold that, as between these two alternatives which he expresses or implies, it is always the first only, and never the second, which is expressed or implied. That is to say, it may be held, that we always only believe or think that an action is right or wrong, and never really know which it is; that, when, therefore, we assert one to be so, we are always merely expressing an opinion or belief, never expressing *knowledge*.

This is a view which is quite tenable, and for which there is a great deal to be said; and it is, I think, certainly liable to be confused with that other, quite untenable, view, that, when a man asserts an action to be right or wrong, all that he *means to assert* is that he thinks it to be so. The two are, in fact, apt to be expressed in exactly the same language. If a man asserts 'Such and such an action was wrong', he is liable to be met by the rejoinder, 'What you really *mean* is that *you think* it was wrong'; and the person who makes this rejoinder will generally only mean by it, that the man does not *know* the action to be wrong, but only believes that it is so: that he is merely expressing his opinion, and has no absolute knowledge on the point. In other words, a man is often loosely said to *mean* by an assertion what, in fact, he is only *expressing* by it; and for this and other reasons the two views we are considering are liable to be confused with one another.

But obviously there is an immense difference between the two. If we only hold the tenable view that no man ever *knows* an action to be right or wrong, but can only *think* it to be so, then, so far from implying the untenable view that to assert an action to be right or wrong is *the same thing* as to assert that we think it to be so, we imply the direct opposite of this. For nobody would maintain that I cannot know *that I think* an action to be right or wrong; and if, therefore, I cannot know that it *is* right or wrong, it follows that there is an immense difference between the assertion that it *is* right or wrong, and the assertion that *I think* it to be so: the former is an assertion, which, according to this view, I can *never* know to be true, whereas the latter is an assertion which I obviously *can* know to be true. The tenable view, therefore, that we can never *know* whether an action is right or wrong, does not in the least support the untenable view that for an action to *be* right or wrong is the same thing as for it to be thought to be so: on the contrary, it is quite inconsistent with it, since it is obvious that we *can* know that certain actions *are thought to be* right and that others *are thought to be* wrong. But yet, I think, it is not uncommon to find the two views combined, and to find one and the same person holding, at the same time, both that we never know whether an action *is* right or wrong, and also that to say that an action *is* right or wrong is the same thing as to say that *it is thought to be* so. The two views ought obviously to be clearly distinguished; and, if they are so distinguished, it becomes, I think, quite plain that the latter must be rejected, if only because, if it were true, the former could not possibly be so.

We have, then, considered in this chapter two different views, namely (1) the view that to say that an action is right or wrong is the same thing as to say that somebody has some *feeling* (or absence of feeling) towards it, and (2) the view that to say that an action is right or wrong is the same thing as to say that somebody *thinks* it to be so. Both these views, when held in certain forms, imply that one and the same action very often is both right and wrong, owing to the fact that different men, and different societies, often do have different and opposite feelings towards, and different and opposite opinions about, the same action. The fact that they imply this is, in itself, an argument against these views; since it seems evident that one and the same action cannot be both right and wrong. But some people may not think that this is evident; and therefore independent objections have been urged against them, which do, I think, show them to be untenable. In the case of the first view, such arguments were only brought against those forms of the view, which do imply that one and the same action is often both right and wrong. The same view may be held in other forms, which do not imply this consequence, and which will therefore be dealt with in the next chapter. But in the case of the second view a general argument was also used, which applies to absolutely all forms in which it may be held.

Even apart from the fact that they lead to the conclusion that one and the same action is often both right and wrong, it is, I think, very important that we should realize, to begin with, that these views are false; because, if they were true, it would follow that we must take an entirely different view as to the whole nature of Ethics, so far as it is concerned with right and wrong, from what has commonly been taken by a majority of writers. If these views were true, the whole business of Ethics, in this department, would merely consist in discovering what feelings and opinions men have actually had about different actions, and why they have had them. A good many writers seem actually to have treated the subject as if this were all that it had to investigate. And of course questions of this sort are not without interest, and are subjects of legitimate curiosity. But such questions only form one special branch of Psychology or Anthropology; and most writers have certainly proceeded on the assumption that the special business of Ethics, and the questions which it has to try to answer, are something quite different from this. They have assumed that the question whether an action *is* right cannot be completely settled by showing that any man or set of men have certain feelings or opinions about it. They would admit that the feelings and opinions of men may, in various ways, have a bearing on the question; but the mere fact that a given man or set of men has a given feeling or opinion can, they would say, never be sufficient, *by itself*, to show that an action is right or wrong.

But the views, which have been considered in this chapter, imply the direct contrary of this: they imply that, when once we have discovered, what men's feelings or opinions actually are, the whole question is finally settled; that there is, in fact, no further question to discuss. I have tried to show that these views are untenable, and I shall, in future, proceed upon the assumption that they are so; as also I shall proceed on the assumption that one and the same action cannot be both right and wrong. And the very fact that *we can* proceed upon these assumptions is an indirect argument in favour of their correctness. For if, whenever we assert an action to be right or wrong, we were merely making an assertion about some man's feelings or opinions, it would be incredible we should be so mistaken as to our own meaning, as to think that a question of right or wrong *cannot* be absolutely settled by showing what men feel and think, and to think that an action *cannot* be both right and wrong. It will be seen that, on these assumptions, we can raise many questions about right and wrong, which seem obviously not to be absurd; and which yet would be quite absurd—would be questions about which we could not hesitate for a moment—if assertions about right and wrong *were* merely assertions about men's feelings and opinions, or if the same action *could* be both right and wrong.

It was stated, at the beginning of the last chapter, that the ethical theory we are considering—the theory stated in the first two chapters— does not maintain with regard to any *class* of voluntary actions, that, if an action of the class in question is once right, any other action of the same class must always be right. And this is true, in the sense in which the statement would, I think, be naturally understood. But it is now important to emphasize that, in a certain sense, the statement is untrue. Our theory does assert that, if any voluntary action is once right, then any other voluntary action which resembled it *in one particular respect* (or rather in a combination of two respects) must always also be right; and since, if we take the word class in the widest possible sense, any set of actions which resemble one another in any respect whatever may be said to form a class, it follows that, in this wide sense, our theory does maintain that there are many classes of action, such that, if an action belonging to one of them is once right, any action belonging to the same class would always be right.

Exactly what our theory does assert under this head cannot, I think, be stated accurately except in rather a complicated way; but it is important to state it as precisely as possible. The precise point is this. This theory asserted, as we saw, that the question whether a voluntary action is right or wrong always depends upon what its *total effects* are, *as compared with* the total effects of all the alternative actions, which we could have done instead. Let us suppose, then, that we have an action X, which is right, and whose total effects are A; and let us suppose that the total effects of all the possible alternative actions would have been respectively B, C, D and E. The precise principle with which we are now concerned may then be stated as follows. Our theory implies, namely, that any action Y which resembled X in *both* the two respects (1) that its total effects were precisely similar to A and (2) that the total effects of all the possible alternatives were precisely similar to B, C, D and E, would necessarily also be right, if X was right, and would necessarily also be wrong, if X was wrong. It is important to emphasize the point that this will only be true of actions which resemble X in *both* these two respects at once. We cannot say that any action Y, whose total effects are precisely similar to those of X, will also be right if X is right. It is absolutely essential that the other condition should also be satisfied; namely, that the total effects of all the possible alternatives should also be precisely similar in both the two cases. For if they were not— if in the case of Y, some alternative was possible, which would have quite different effects, from any that would have been produced by any alternative that was possible in the case of X—then, according to our theory, it is possible that the total effects of this other alternative would be *intrinsically better* than those of Y, and in that case Y will be wrong, even though its total effects are precisely similar to those of X and X was right. *Both* conditions must, therefore, be satisfied simultaneously. But our theory does imply that any action which does resemble another in *both* these two respects at once, must be right if the first be right, and wrong if the first be wrong.

This is the precise principle with which we are now concerned. It may perhaps be stated more conveniently in the form in which it was stated in the second chapter: namely, that if it is *ever* right to do an action whose total effects are A in preference to one whose total effects are B, it must always be right to do any action whose total effects are precisely similar to A in preference to one whose total effects are precisely similar to B. It is also, I think, what is commonly meant by saying, simply, that the question whether an action is right or wrong always depends upon its total effects or consequences; but this will not do as an accurate statement of it, because, as we shall see, it may be held that right and wrong do, in a sense, always depend upon an action's total consequences and yet that this principle is untrue. It is also sometimes expressed by saying that if an action is once right, any precisely similar action, done in circumstances which are also precisely similar in all respects, must be right too. But this is both too narrow and too wide. It is too narrow, because our principle does not confine itself to an assertion about *precisely similar* actions. Our principle asserts that any action Y, whose *effects* are precisely similar to those of another X, will be right, if X is right, provided the effects of all the alternatives possible in the two cases are also precisely similar, even though Y itself is *not* precisely similar to X, but utterly different from it. And it is too wide, because it does not follow from the fact that two actions are both precisely similar in themselves and also done in precisely similar circumstances, that their effects must also be precisely similar. This does, of course, follow, *so long as the laws of nature remain the same*. But if we suppose the laws of nature to change, or if we conceive a Universe in which different laws of nature hold from those which hold in this one, then plainly a precisely similar action done in precisely similar circumstances might yet have *different* total effects. According to our principle, therefore, the statement that any two precisely similar actions, done in precisely similar circumstances, must both be right, if one is right, though true as applied to this Universe, provided (as is commonly supposed) the laws of nature cannot change, is not true *absolutely unconditionally*. But our principle asserts *absolutely unconditionally* that if it is once right to prefer a set of total effects A to another set B, it must always, in any conceivable Universe, be right to prefer a set precisely similar to A to a set precisely similar to B.

This, then, is a second very fundamental principle, which our theory asserts—a principle which is, in a sense, concerned with *classes* of actions, and not merely with particular actions. And in asserting this principle also it seems to me that our theory is right. But many different views have been held, which, while admitting that one and the same action cannot be both right and wrong, yet assert or imply that this second principle is untrue. And I propose in this chapter to deal with those among them which resemble the theories dealt with in the last chapter in one particular respect—namely, that they depend upon some view as to the *meaning* of the word 'right' or as to the meaning of the word 'good'.

And, first of all, we may briefly mention a theory, which is very similar to some of those dealt with in the last chapter and which is, I think, often confused with them, but which yet differs from them in one very important respect. This is the theory that to say that an action is right or wrong is the same thing as to say that a majority of *all* mankind have, more often than not, some particular feeling (or absence of feeling) towards actions of the class to which it belongs. This theory differs from those considered in the last chapter, because it does not imply that one and the same action ever actually is both right and wrong. For, however much the feelings of different men and different societies may differ at different times, yet, if we take strictly a majority of *all* mankind at *all* times past, present and future, any class of action which is, for instance, generally approved by such an absolute majority of all mankind, will *not* also be disapproved by an absolute majority of *all* mankind, although it may be disapproved by a majority of any one society, or by a majority of all the men living at any one period. This proposal, therefore, to say that, when we assert an action to be right or wrong, we are making an assertion about the feelings of an absolute majority of *all* mankind does not conflict with the principle that one and the same action cannot be both right and wrong. It allows us to say that any particular action always is either right or wrong, in spite of the fact that different men and different societies may feel differently towards actions of that class at the same or different times. What it does conflict with is the principle we are now considering. Since it implies that if a majority of mankind did *not* happen to have a particular feeling towards actions of one class A, it *would* not be right to prefer actions of this class to those of another class B, even though the effects of A and B, respectively, might be precisely similar to what they now are. It implies, that is to say, that in a Universe in which there were no men, or in which the feelings of the majority were different from what they are in this one, it might *not* be right to prefer one total set of effects A to another B, even though in this Universe it *is* always right to prefer them.

Now I do not know if this theory has ever been expressly held; but some philosophers have certainly argued *as if* it were true. Great pains have, for instance, been taken to show that mankind are, *in general*, pleased with actions which lead to a maximum of pleasure, and displeased with those which lead to less than a maximum; and the proof that this is so has been treated as if it were, at the same time, a proof that it is *always* right to do what leads to a maximum of pleasure, and wrong to do what leads to less than a maximum. But obviously, unless to show that mankind are *generally* pleased with a particular sort of action is *the same thing* as to show that that sort of action is *always* right, some independent proof is needed to show that what mankind are generally pleased with *is* always right.

And some of those who have used this argument do not seem to have seen that any such proof is needed. So soon as we recognize quite clearly that to say that an action is right is *not* the same thing as to say that mankind are generally pleased with it, it becomes obvious that to show that mankind are generally pleased with a particular sort of action is *not* sufficient to show that it is right. And hence it is, I think, fair to say that those who have argued as if it *were* sufficient, have argued *as if* to say that an action is right were the same thing as saying that mankind are generally pleased with it; although, perhaps, if this assumption had been expressly put before them, they would have rejected it.

We may therefore say, I think, that the theory that to call an action right or wrong is the same thing as to say that an absolute majority of all mankind have some particular feeling (or absence of feeling) towards actions of that kind, has often been assumed, even if it has not been expressly held. And it is, therefore, perhaps worth while to point out that it is exposed to exactly the same objection as two of the theories dealt with in the last chapter. The objection is that it is quite certain, as a matter of fact, that a man may have no doubt that an action is right, even where he *does* doubt whether an absolute majority of all mankind have a particular feeling (or absence of feeling) towards it, no matter what feeling we take. And what this shows is that, whatever he is thinking, when he thinks the action to be right, he is not merely thinking that a majority of mankind have any particular feeling towards it. Even, therefore, if it be true that what is approved or liked by an absolute majority of mankind is, *as a matter of fact,* always right (and this we are not disputing), it is quite certain that to say that it is right is not *the same thing* as to say that it is thus approved. And with this we come to the end of a certain type of theories with regard to the meaning of the words 'right' and and 'wrong'. We are now entitled to the conclusion that, whatever the meaning of these words may be, it is not identical with any assertion whatever about either the feelings or the thoughts of *men*—neither those of any particular man, nor those of any particular society, nor those of some man or other, nor those of mankind as a whole. To predicate of an action that it is right or wrong is to predicate of it something quite different from the mere fact that any man or set of men have any particular feeling towards, or opinion about, it.

But there are some philosophers who, while feeling the strongest objection to the view that one and the same action can ever be both right and wrong, and also to any view which implies that the question whether an action is right or wrong depends in any way upon what men—even the majority of men—actually feel or think about it, yet seem to be so strongly convinced that to call an action right *must* be merely to make an assertion about the attitude of *some* being towards it, that they have adopted the view that there is some being other than any man or set of men, whose attitude towards the same action or class of actions never changes, and that, when we assert actions to be right or wrong, what we are doing is merely to make an assertion about the attitude of this non-human being. And theories of this type are the next which I wish to consider.

Those who have held some theory of this type have, I think, generally held that what we mean by calling an action right or wrong is not that the non-human being in question has or has not some *feeling* towards actions of the class to which it belongs, but that it has or has not towards them one of the mental attitudes which we call *willing* or *forbidding*; a kind of mental attitude with which we are all familiar, and which is not generally classed under the head of feelings, but under a quite separate head. To *forbid* actions of a certain class is the same thing as to will or command that they should *not* be done. And the view generally held is, I think, that to say that an action *ought* to be done, is the same thing as to say that it belongs to a class which the non-human being *wills* or commands; to say that it is *right*, is to say that it belongs to a class which the non-human being does *not* forbid; and to say that it is *wrong* or ought not to be done is to say that it belongs to a class which the non-human being *does* forbid. All assertions about right and wrong are, accordingly, by theories of this type, identified with assertions about the *will* of some non-human being. And there are two obvious reasons why we should hold that, if judgements of right and wrong are judgements about any mental attitude at all, they are judgements about the mental attitude which we call *willing*, rather than about any of those which we call *feelings*.

The first is that the notion which we express by the word 'right' seems to be obviously closely connected with that which we express by the word 'ought,' in the manner explained in Chapter I (pp. 13-16); and that there are many usages of language which seem to suggest that the word 'ought' expresses a command. The very name of the Ten Commandments is a familiar instance, and so is the language in which they are expressed. Everybody understands these Commandments as assertions to the effect that certain actions *ought*, and that others *ought not* to be done. But yet they are called 'Commandments', and if we look at what they actually say we find such expressions as 'Thou shalt do no murder', Thou shalt not steal'—expressions which are obviously equivalent to the imperatives, 'Do no murder', 'Do not steal', and which strictly, therefore, should express commands. For this reason alone it is very natural to suppose that the word 'ought' *always* expresses a command. And there is yet another reason in favour of the same supposition—namely, that the fact that actions of a certain class ought or ought not to be done is often called 'a moral *law*', a name which naturally suggests that such facts are in some way analogous to 'laws', in the legal sense—the sense in which we talk of the laws of England or of any other country. But if we look to see what is meant by saying that any given thing is, in this sense, 'part of the law' of a given community, there are a good many facts in favour of the view that nothing can be part of the law of any community, unless it has either itself been willed by some person or persons having the necessary authority over that community, or can be deduced from something which has been so willed. It is, indeed, not at all an easy thing to define what is meant by *'having the necessary authority'*, or, in other words, to say in what relation a person or set of persons must stand to a community, if it is to be true that nothing can be a law of that community except what these persons have willed, or what can be deduced from something which they have willed. But still it may be true that there always is some person or set of persons whose will or consent is necessary to make a law a law. And whether this is so or not, it does seem to be the case that every law, which is the law of any community, is, in a certain sense, *dependent* upon the human will. This is true in the sense that, in the case of every law whatever, there always are *some* men, who, by performing certain acts of will, could make it cease to be the law; and also that, in the case of anything whatever which is *not* the law, there always are *some* men, who, by performing certain acts of will, could make it be the law: though, of course, any given set of men who could effect the change in the case of some laws, could very often *not* effect it in the case of others, but in their case another set of men would be required: and, of course, in some cases the number of men whose co-operation would be required would be very large. It does seem, therefore, as if laws, in the legal sense, were essentially dependent on the human will; and this fact naturally suggests that moral laws also are dependent on the will of some being.

These are, I think, the two chief reasons which have led people to suppose that moral judgements are judgements about the *will*, rather than about the *feelings*, of some being or beings. And there are, of course, the same objections to supposing, in the case of *moral* laws, that the being or beings in question can be any man or set of men, as there are to the supposition that judgements about right and wrong can be merely judgements about men's feelings and opinions. In this way, therefore, there has naturally arisen the view we are now considering—the view that to say of an action that it ought to be done, or is right, or ought not to be done, is the same thing as to say that it belongs to a class of actions which has been commanded, or permitted, or forbidden by some *non-human* being. Different views have, of course, been taken as to who or what the non-human being is. One of the simplest is that it is God: that is to say, that, when we call an action wrong, we mean to say that God has forbidden it. But other philosophers have supposed that it is a being which may be called 'Reason', or one called 'The Practical Reason', or one called 'The Pure Will', or one called 'The Universal Will', or one called 'The True Self'. In some cases, the beings called by these names have been supposed to be merely 'faculties' of the human mind, or some other entity, resident in, or forming a part of, the minds of all men. And, where this is the case, it may seem unfair to call these supposed entities 'non-human'. But all that I mean by calling them this is to emphasize the fact that even if they are faculties of, or entities resident in, the human mind, they are, at least, not *human beings*—that is to say, they are not *men*—either any one particular man or any set of men. For *ex hypothesi* they are beings which can never will what is wrong, whereas it is admitted that all *men* can, and sometimes do, will what is wrong. No doubt sometimes, when philosophers speak as if they believed in the existence of beings of this kind, they are speaking metaphorically and do not really hold any such belief. Thus a philosopher may often speak of an ethical truth as 'a dictate of Reason', without really meaning to imply that there is any faculty or part of our mind which invariably leads us right and never leads us wrong. But I think there is no doubt that such language is not always metaphorical. The view is held that whenever I judge truly or will rightly, there really is a something in me which does these things—the same something on every different occasion; and that this something *never* judges falsely or wills wrongly: so that, when I judge falsely and will wrongly, it is a *different* something in me which does so.

Now it may seem to many people that the most serious objection to views of this kind is that it is, to say the least, extremely doubtful whether there is any being, such as they suppose to exist—any being, who never wills what is wrong but always only what is right; and I think myself that, in all probability there is no such being—neither a God, nor any being such as philosophers have called by the names I have mentioned. But adequately to discuss the reasons for and against supposing that there is one would take us far too long. And fortunately it is unnecessary for our present purpose; since the only question we need to answer is whether, even supposing there is such a being, who commands all that ought to be done and only what ought to be done, and forbids all that is wrong and only what is wrong, what we *mean* by saying that an action ought or ought not to be done can possibly be merely *that* this being commands it or forbids it. And it seems to me there is a conclusive argument against supposing that this can be all that we mean, even if there really is, in fact, such a being.

The argument is simply that, whether there is such a being or not, there certainly are many people who do not believe that there is one, and that such people, in spite of not believing in its existence, can nevertheless continue to believe that actions are right and wrong. But this would be quite impossible if the view we are considering were true. According to that view, to believe that an action is wrong is *the same thing* as to believe that it is forbidden by one of these non-human beings; so that any one whatever who ever does believe that an action is wrong is, *ipso facto*, believing in the existence of such a being. It maintains, therefore, that everybody who believes that actions are right or wrong does, as a matter of fact, believe in the existence of one of these beings. And this contention seems to be plainly contrary to fact. It might, indeed, be urged that when we say there are some people who *do not* believe in any of these beings, all that is really true is that there are some people who *think* they do not believe in them; while, in fact, everybody really does. But it is surely impossible seriously to maintain that, in all cases, they are so mistaken as to the nature of their own beliefs. But if so, then it follows absolutely that even if wrong actions always are in fact forbidden by some non-human being, yet to say that they are wrong is not identical with saying that they are so forbidden.

And it is important also, as an argument against views of this class, to insist upon the reason why they contradict the principle which we are considering in this chapter. They contradict this principle, because they imply that there is absolutely *no* class of actions of which we can say that it always *would,* in any conceivable Universe, be right or wrong. They imply this because that *if* the non-human being, whom they suppose to exist, did not exist, nothing would be right or wrong. Thus, for instance, if it is held that to call an action wrong is *the same thing* as to say that it is forbidden by God, it will follow that, if God did not exist, nothing would be wrong; and hence that we cannot possibly hold that God forbids what is wrong, *because* it is wrong. We must hold, on the contrary, that the wrongness of what is wrong consists simply and solely in the fact that God does forbid it—a view to which many even of those, who believe that what is wrong is in fact forbidden by God, will justly feel an objection.

For these reasons, it seems to me, we may finally conclude that, when we assert any action to be right or wrong, we are not merely making an assertion about the attitude of mind towards it of any being or set of beings whatever—no matter what attitude of mind we take to be the one in question, whether one of feeling or thinking or willing, and no matter what being or beings we take, whether human or non-human: and that hence no proof to the effect that any particular being or set of beings has or has not a particular attitude of mind towards an action is sufficient to prove that the action really is right or wrong.

But there are many philosophers who fully admit this—who admit that the predicates which we denote by the words 'right' and 'wrong' do not consist in the having of any relation whatever to any being's feelings or thoughts or will; and who will even go further than this and admit that the question whether an action is right or wrong does depend, in a sense, solely upon its consequences, namely, in the sense, that no action ever can be right, if it was possible for the agent to do something else which would have had *better* total consequences; but who, while admitting all this, nevertheless maintain that to call one set of consequences *better* than another is the same thing as to say that the one set is related to some mind or minds in a way in which the other is not related. That is to say, while admitting that to call an action right or wrong is *not* merely to assert that some particular mental attitude is taken up towards it, they hold that to call a thing 'good' or 'bad' *is* merely to assert this. And of course, if it be true that no action ever can be right unless its total effects are as *good* as possible, then this view as to the meaning of the words 'good' and 'bad' will contradict the principle we are considering in this chapter as effectively as if the corresponding view be held about the meaning of the words 'right' and 'wrong'. For if, in saying that one set of effects A is *better* than another B we merely mean to say that A has a relation to some mind or minds which B has *not* got, then it will follow that a set of effects precisely similar to A will *not* be better than a set precisely similar to B, if they do not happen to have the required relations to any mind. And hence it will follow that even though, on one occasion or in one Universe, it is right to prefer A to B, yet, on another occasion or in another Universe, it may quite easily *not* be right to prefer a set of effects precisely similar to A to a set precisely similar to B.

For this reason, the view that the meaning of the words 'good' and 'bad' is merely that some being has some mental attitude towards the thing so called, may constitute a fatal objection to the principle which we are considering. It will, indeed, only do so, if we admit that it must always be right to do what has the *best* possible total effects. But it may be held that this is self-evident, and many persons, who hold this view with regard to the meaning of 'good' and 'bad' would, I think, be inclined to admit that it is so. Hence it becomes important to consider this new objection to our principle.

This view that by calling a thing 'good' or 'bad' we merely mean that some being or beings have a certain mental attitude towards it, has been even more commonly held than the corresponding view with regard to 'right' and 'wrong'; and it may be held in as many different forms. Thus it may be held that to say that a thing is 'good' is the same thing as to say that somebody *thinks* it is good—a view which may be refuted by the same general argument which was used in the case of the corresponding view about 'right' and 'wrong'. Again it may be held that each man when he calls a thing 'good' or 'bad' merely means that *he himself* thinks it to be so or has some feeling towards it; a view from which it will follow, as in the case of right and wrong, that no two men can ever differ in opinion as to whether a thing is good or bad. Again, also, in most of the forms, in which it can be held, it will certainly follow that one and the same thing can be *both* good and bad; since, whatever pair of mental attitudes or single mental attitude we take, it seems as certain here, as in the case of right and wrong, that different men will sometimes have different mental attitudes towards the same thing. This has, however, been very often disputed in the case of one particular mental attitude, which deserves to be specially mentioned.

One of the chief differences between the views which have been held with regard to the meaning of 'good' and 'bad', and those which have been held with regard to the meaning of 'right' and 'wrong', is that in the former case it has been very often held that what we mean by calling a thing 'good' is that it is *desired,* or desired in some particular way; and this attitude of 'desire' is one that I did not mention in the case of 'right' and 'wrong' because, so far as I know, nobody has ever held that to call an action 'right' is the same thing as to say that it is desired. But the commonest of all views with regard to the meaning of the word 'good', is that to call a thing good is to say that it is desired, or desired for its own sake; and curiously enough this view has been used as an argument in favour of the very theory stated in our first two chapters, on the ground that no man ever desires (or desires for its own sake) anything at all except *pleasure* (or *his own* pleasure), and that hence, since 'good' means 'desired', any set of effects which contains more pleasure *must* always be better than one which contains less. Of course, even if it were true that no *man* ever desires anything except pleasure, it would not really follow, as this argument assumes, that a whole which contains more pleasure must *always* be better than one which contains less. On the contrary, the very opposite would follow; since it would follow that *if* any beings did happen to desire something other than pleasure (and we can easily conceive that some might) then wholes which contained more pleasure might easily *not* always be better than those which contained less. But it is now generally recognized that it is a complete mistake to suppose even that *men* desire nothing but pleasure, or even that they desire nothing else for its own sake. And, whether it is so or not, the question is irrelevant to our present purpose, which is to find some quite general arguments to show that to call a thing 'good' is, in any case, *not* the same thing as merely to say that it is desired or desired for its own sake, nor yet that any other mental attitude whatever is taken up towards it. What arguments can we find to show this?

One point should be carefully noticed to begin with; namely, that we have no need to show that when we call a thing 'good' we *never* mean simply that somebody has some mental attitude towards it.

There are many reasons for thinking that the word 'good' is ambiguous—that we use it in different senses on different occasions; and, if so, it is quite possible that, in *some* of its uses, it should stand merely for the assertion that somebody has some feeling or some other mental attitude towards the thing called 'good', although, in *other* uses, it does not. We are not, therefore, concerned to show that it may not *sometimes* merely stand for this; all that we need to show is that *sometimes* it does not. For what we have to do is merely to meet the argument that, if we assert, 'It would always be wrong to prefer a *worse* set of total consequences to a *better*', we *must*, in this proposition, mean merely by 'worse' and 'better', consequences to which a certain mental attitude is taken up—a conclusion from which it would follow that, even though a set of consequences A was *once* better than a set B, a set precisely similar to A would not always necessarily be better than a set precisely similar to B. And obviously all that we need to do, to show this, is to show that *some* sense can be given to the words 'better' and 'worse', quite other than this; or, in other words, that to call a thing 'good' does not *always* mean merely that some mental attitude is taken up towards it.

It will be best, therefore, in order to make the problem definite, to concentrate attention upon one particular usage of the word, in which it seems clearly not to mean this. And I will take as an example that usage in which we make judgements of what was called in Chapter II '*intrinsic* value'; that is to say, where we judge, concerning a particular state of things that it would be worth while—would be 'a good thing'—that that state of things should exist, *even if nothing else were to exist besides,* either at the same time or afterwards. We do not, of course, so constantly make judgements of this kind, as we do some other judgements about the goodness of things. But we certainly *can* make them, and it seems quite clear that we mean *something* by them. We *can* consider with regard to any particular state of things whether it would be worth while that it should exist, even if there were absolutely nothing else in the Universe besides; whether, for instance, it would have been worth while that the Universe, as it has existed up till now, should have existed, even if absolutely nothing were to follow, but its existence were to be cut short at the present moment: we *can* consider whether the existence of such a Universe would have been better than nothing, or whether it would have been just as good that nothing at all should ever have existed. In the case of such judgements as these it seems to me there are strong reasons for holding that we are not merely making an assertion either about our own or about anybody else's attitude of mind towards the state of things in question. And if we can show this, in this one case, that is sufficient for our purpose.

What, then, are the reasons for holding it?

I think we should distinguish two different cases, according to the *kind* of attitude of mind about which it is supposed that we are making an assertion.

If it is held that what we are asserting is merely that the state of things in question is one that we or somebody else is *pleased* at the idea of, or one that is or would be *desired* or *desired for its own sake* (and these are the views that seem to be most commonly held), the following argument seems to me to be conclusive against all views of this type. Namely, a man certainly can believe with regard to a given thing or state of things, that the idea of it *does* please somebody, and *is* desired, and even desired for its own sake, and yet *not* believe that it would be at all worth while that it should exist, if it existed quite alone. He may even believe that it would be a positively bad thing— *worse* than nothing—that it should exist quite alone, in spite of the fact that he knows that it is desired and strongly desired for its own sake, even by himself. That some men can and do make such judgements—that they can and do judge that things which they themselves desire or are pleased with, are nevertheless intrinsically bad (that is to say *would* be bad, quite apart from their consequences, and even if they existed quite alone) is, I think, undeniable; and no doubt men make this judgement even more frequently with regard to things which are desired by others. And if this is so, then it shows conclusively that to judge that a thing is intrinsically good is not the same thing as to judge that some man is pleased with it or desires it or desires it for its own sake. Of course, it may be held that anybody who makes such a judgement is wrong: that, as a matter of fact, anything whatever which is desired, always is intrinsically good. But that is not the question. We are not disputing for the moment that this may be so as *a matter of fact*. All that we are trying to show is that, even if it is so, yet, to say that a thing is intrinsically good is not *the same thing* as to say that it is desired: and this follows absolutely, if even in a single case, a man believes that a thing *is* desired and yet does *not* believe that it is intrinsically good.

But I am not sure that this argument will hold against all forms in which the view might be held, although it does hold against those in which it is most commonly held. There are, I think, feelings with regard to which it is much more plausible to hold that to believe that they are felt towards a given thing is the same thing as to believe that the thing is intrinsically good, than it is to hold this with regard to the mere feeling of pleasure, or desire, or desire of a thing 'for its own sake'. For instance, it may, so far as I can see, be true that there really is some very special feeling of such a nature that any man who knows that he himself or anybody else really feels it towards any state of things cannot doubt that the state of things in question is intrinsically good. If this be so, then the last argument will not hold against the view that when we call a thing intrinsically good we may mean merely that *this special feeling* is felt towards it. And against any such view, if it were held, the only obvious argument I can find is that it is surely plain that, even if the special feeling in question had *not* been felt by any one towards the given state of things, yet the state of things *would* have been intrinsically good.

But, in order fully to make plain the force of this argument, it is necessary to guard against one misunderstanding, which is very commonly made and which is apt to obscure the whole question which we are now discussing. That is to say, we are not now urging that anything would be any good at all, unless somebody had some feeling towards *something;* nor are we urging that there are not many things, which *are* good, in *one* sense of the word, and which yet would not be any good at all unless somebody had some feeling towards them. On the contrary, both these propositions, which are very commonly held, seem to me to be perfectly true. I think it is true that no whole can be intrinsically good, unless it *contains* some feeling towards *something* as a part of itself; and true also that, in a very important sense of the word 'good' (though not in the sense to which I have given the name 'intrinsically good'), many things which *are* good would not be good, unless somebody had some feeling towards them. We must, therefore, clearly distinguish the question whether these things are so, from the question which we are now discussing. The question we are now discussing is merely whether, granted that nothing can be intrinsically good unless it *contains* some feeling, a thing which *is* thus good and *does* contain this feeling cannot be good without anybody's needing to have *another* feeling towards *it*. The point may be simply illustrated by taking the case of pleasure. Let us suppose, for the moment, that nothing can be intrinsically good unless it contains some pleasure, and that every whole which contains more pleasure than pain is intrinsically good. The question we are now discussing is merely whether, supposing this to be so, any whole which did contain more pleasure than pain, *would* not be good, even if nobody had *any further feeling* towards it. It seems to me quite plain that it would be so. But if so, then, to say that a state of things is intrinsically good cannot possibly be the same thing as to say that anybody has any kind of feeling towards *it,* even though no state of things can be intrinsically good unless it *contains* some feeling towards *something.*

But, after all, I do not know whether the strongest argument against any view which asserts that to call a thing 'good' is the same thing as to say that some mental attitude is taken up towards it, does not merely consist in the fact that two propositions about 'right' and 'wrong' are self-evident: namely (1) that, if it were once the duty of any being, who *knew* that the total effects of one action would be A, and those of another B, to choose the action which produced A rather than that which produced B, it must *always* be the duty of any being who had to choose between two actions, one of which he knew would have total effects precisely similar to A and the other total effects precisely similar to B, to choose the former rather than the latter, and (2) that it must always be the duty of any being who had to choose between two actions, one of which he *knew* would have *better* total effects than the other, to choose the former. From these two propositions taken together it absolutely follows that if one set of total effects A is once *better* than another B, any set precisely similar to A must *always* be better than any set precisely similar to B. And, if so, then 'better' and 'worse' *cannot* stand for any relation to any attitude of mind; since we cannot be entitled to say that if a given attitude is once taken up towards A and B, the same attitude would always *necessarily* be taken up towards any pair of wholes precisely similar to A and B.

V RESULTS THE TEST OF RIGHT
AND WRONG

In our last chapter we began considering objections to one very fundamental principle, which is pre-supposed by the theory stated in the first two chapters—a principle which may be summed up in the two propositions (1) that the question whether an action is right or wrong always depends upon its *total* consequences, and (2) that if it is once right to prefer one set of *total* consequences, A, to another set, B, it must always be right to prefer any set precisely similar to A to any set precisely similar to B. The objections to this principle, which we considered in the last chapter, rested on certain views with regard to the meaning of the words 'right' and 'good'. But there remain several other quite independent objections, which may be urged against it even if we reject those views. That is to say, there are objections which may and would be urged against it by many people who accept both of the two propositions which I was trying to establish in the last chapter, namely (1) that to call an action 'right' or 'wrong' is not the same thing as to say that any being whatever has towards it any mental attitude whatever; and (2) that if any given whole is once intrinsically good or bad, any whole precisely similar to it must always be intrinsically good or bad in precisely the same degree. And in the present chapter I wish briefly to consider what seem to me to be the most important of these remaining objections.

All of them are directed against the view that right and wrong do always depend upon an action's *actual* consequences or results. This may be denied for several different reasons; and I shall try to state fairly the chief among these reasons, and to point out why they do not seem to be conclusive.

In the first place, it may be said that, by laying down the principle that right and wrong depend upon consequences, we are doing away with the distinction between what is a *duty* and what is merely *expedient*; and between what is *wrong* and what is merely *inexpedient*. People certainly do commonly make a distinction between duty and expediency. And it may be said that the very meaning of calling an action 'expedient' is to say that it will produce the best consequences possible under the circumstances. If, therefore, we also say that an action is a *duty*, whenever and only when it produces the best possible consequences, it may seem that nothing is left to distinguish duty from expediency.

Now, as against this objection, it is important to point out, first of all, that, even if we admit that to call an action expedient is the same thing as to say that it produces the best possible consequences, our principle still does not compel us to hold that to call an action expedient is *the same thing* as to call it a duty. All that it does compel us to hold is that whatever is expedient is always *also* a duty, and that whatever is a duty is always *also* expedient. That is to say, it *does* maintain that duty and expediency *coincide*; but it does *not* maintain that the meaning of the two words is the same. It is, indeed, quite plain, I think, that the meaning of the two words is *not* the same; for, if it were, then it would be a mere tautology to say that it is always our duty to do what will have the best possible consequences. Our theory does not, therefore, do away with the distinction between the *meaning* of the words 'duty' and 'expediency'; it only maintains that both will always apply to the same actions.

But, no doubt, what is meant by many who urge this objection is to deny this. What they mean to say is not merely that to call an action expedient is a different thing from calling it a duty, but also that sometimes what *is* expedient is *wrong*, and what *is* a duty is inexpedient. This is a view which is undoubtedly often held; people often speak as if there often were an actual conflict between duty and expediency. But many of the cases in which it would be commonly held that there is such a conflict may, I think, be explained by supposing that when we call an action 'expedient' we do not always mean quite strictly that its *total* consequences, taking absolutely *everything* into account, are the best possible. It is by no means clear that we do always mean this. We may, perhaps, sometimes mean merely that the action is expedient for some particular purpose; and sometimes that it is expedient in the interests of the agent, though not so on the whole. But if we only mean this, our theory, of course, does *not* compel us to maintain that the expedient *is* always a duty, and duty always expedient. It only compels us to maintain this, if 'expedient' be understood in the strictest and fullest sense, as meaning that, when *absolutely all* the consequences are taken into account, they will be found to be the best possible. And if this be clearly understood, then most people, I think, will be reluctant to admit that it can ever be really inexpedient to do our duty, or that what is really and truly expedient, in this strict sense, can ever be wrong.

But, no doubt, some people may still maintain that it is or may be sometimes our duty to do actions which will *not* have the best possible consequences, and sometimes also positively wrong, to do actions which will. And the chief reason why this is held is, I think, the following.

It is, in fact, very commonly held indeed that there are certain specific kinds of action which are absolutely always right, and others which are absolutely always wrong. Different people will, indeed, take different views as to exactly what kinds of action have this character. A rule which will be offered by one set of persons as a rule to which there is absolutely no exception will be rejected by others, as obviously admitting of exceptions; but these will generally, in their turn, maintain that some other rule, which they can mention, really has no exceptions. Thus there are enormous numbers of people who would agree that *some rule or other* (and generally more than one) ought *absolutely always* to be obeyed; although probably there is not one single rule which *all* the persons who maintain this would agree upon. Thus, for instance, some people might maintain that murder (defined in some particular way) is an act which ought absolutely *never* to be committed; or that to act *justly* is a rule which ought absolutely always to be obeyed; and similarly it might be suggested with regard to many other kinds of action, that they are actions, which it is either *always* our duty, or *always* wrong to do.

But once we assert with regard to any rule of this kind that it *is absolutely always* our duty to obey it, it is easy and natural to take one further step and to say that it *would* always be our duty to obey it, *whatever* the consequences might be. Of course, this further step does not necessarily and logically follow from the mere position that there are some kinds of action which ought, *in fact,* absolutely always to be done or avoided. For it is just possible that there are some kinds which do, as a matter of fact, absolutely always produce the best possible consequences, and other kinds which absolutely never do so. And there is a strong tendency among persons who hold the first position to hold that, as a matter of fact, this is the case: that right actions always do, as a matter of fact, produce the best possible results, and wrong actions never. Thus even those who would assent to the maxim that 'Justice should always be done, though the heavens should fall', will generally be disposed to believe that justice never will, in fact, cause the heavens to fall, but will rather be always the best means of upholding them. And similarly those who say that 'you should never do evil that good may come', though their maxim seems to imply that good *may* sometimes come from doing wrong, would yet be very loth to admit that, by doing wrong, you ever would *really* produce better consequences *on the whole* than if you had acted rightly instead. Or again, those who say 'that the end will never justify the means', though they certainly imply that certain ways of acting would be always wrong, *whatever* advantages might be secured by them, yet, I think, would be inclined to deny that the advantages to be obtained by acting wrongly ever do *really* outweigh those to be obtained by acting rightly, if we take into account absolutely *all* the consequences of each course.

Those, therefore, who hold that certain specific ways of acting are absolutely always right, and others absolutely always wrong, do, I think, generally hold that the former do also, as a matter of fact, absolutely always produce the best results, and the latter never. But, for the reasons given at the beginning of Chapter III, it is, I think, very unlikely that this belief can be justified. The total results of an action always depend, not merely on the specific nature of the action, but on the circumstances in which it is done; and the circumstances vary so greatly that it is, in most cases, extremely unlikely that any particular kind of action will *absolutely* always, in absolutely all circumstances, either produce or fail to produce the best possible results. For this reason, if we do take the view that right and wrong depend upon consequences, we must, I think, be prepared to doubt whether any particular kind of action whatever is absolutely always right or absolutely always wrong. For instance, however we define 'murder', it is unlikely that absolutely *no* case will ever occur in which it would be right to commit a murder; and, however we define 'justice', it is unlikely that *no* case will ever occur in which it would be right to do an injustice. No doubt it may be possible to define actions of which it is true that, in an *immense* majority of cases, it is right or wrong to perform them; and perhaps *some* rules of this kind might be found to which there are really *no* exceptions. But in the case of most of the ordinary moral rules, it seems extremely unlikely that obedience to them will *absolutely always* produce the best possible results. And most persons who realize this would, I think, be disposed to give up the view that they ought absolutely *always* to be obeyed. They would be content to accept them as *general* rules, to which there are very few exceptions, without pretending that they are absolutely universal.

But, no doubt, there may be some persons who will hold, in the case of some particular rule or set of rules, that even if obedience to it does in some cases *not* produce the best possible consequences, yet we ought even in these cases to obey it. It may seem to them that they really do know certain rules, which ought *absolutely always* to be obeyed, *whatever* the consequences may be, and even, therefore, if the total consequences are not the best possible. They may, for instance, take quite seriously the assertion that justice ought to be done, even though the heavens should fall, as meaning that, *however* bad the consequences of doing an act of justice might in some circumstances be, yet it always would be our duty to do it. And such a view does necessarily contradict our principle; since, whether it be true or not that an act of injustice ever actually could in this world produce the best possible consequences, it is certainly possible to *conceive* circumstances in which it would do so. I doubt whether those who believe in the absolute universality of certain moral rules do generally thus distinguish quite clearly between the question whether disobedience to the rule ever *could* produce the best possible consequences, and the question whether, *if* it did, then disobedience would be wrong. They would generally be disposed to argue that it never really *could*. But some persons might perhaps hold that, even if it did, yet disobedience would be wrong. And if this view be quite clearly held, there is, so far as I can see, absolutely no way of refuting it except by appealing to the self-evidence of the principle that if we *knew* that the effect of a given action really would be to make the world, as a whole, *worse* than it would have been if we had acted differently, it certainly would be wrong for us to do that action. Those who say that certain rules ought *absolutely always* to be obeyed, *whatever* the consequences may be, are logically bound to deny this; for by saying '*whatever* the consequences may be', they do imply '*even if* the world as a whole were the worse because of our action'. It seems to me to be self-evident that knowingly to do an action which would make the world, on the whole, really and truly *worse* than if we had acted differently, must always be wrong. And if this be admitted, then it absolutely disposes of the view that there are any kinds of action whatever, which it *would* always be our duty to do or to avoid, *whatever* the consequences might be.

For this reason it seems to me we must reject this particular objection to the view that right and wrong always depend upon consequences; namely, the objection that there are certain *kinds* of action which ought absolutely always and quite unconditionally to be done or avoided. But there still remain two other objections, which are so commonly held, that it is worth while to consider them.

The first is the objection that right and wrong depend neither upon the nature of the action, nor upon its consequences, but partly, or even entirely, upon the *motive* or *motives* from which it is done. By the view that it depends *partly* upon the motives, I mean the view that no action can be *really* right, unless it be done from some one motive, or some one of a set of motives, which are supposed to be good; but that the being done from such a motive is not sufficient, *by itself*, to make an action right: that the action, if it is to be right, must always *also* either produce the best possible consequences, or be distinguished by some other characteristic. And this view, therefore, will not necessarily contradict our principle so far as it asserts that no action can be right, *unless* it produces the best possible consequences: it only contradicts that part of it which asserts that *every* action which does produce them is right. But the view has sometimes been held, I think, that right and wrong depend *entirely* upon motives: that is to say, that not only is no action right, *unless* it be done from a good motive, but also that *any* action which is done from some one motive or some one of a set of motives is always right, whatever its consequences may be and whatever it may be like in other respects. And this view, of course, will contradict both parts of our principle; since it not only implies that an action, which produces the best possible consequences may be wrong, but also that an action may be right, in spite of failing to produce them.

In favour of both these views it may be urged that in our moral judgements we actually do, and ought to, take account of motives; and indeed that it marks a great advance in morality when men do begin to attach importance to motives and are not guided exclusively, in their praise or blame, by the 'external' nature of the act done or by its consequences. And all this may be fully admitted. It is quite certain that when a man does an action which has bad consequences from a good motive, we do tend to judge him differently from a man who does a similar action from a bad one; and also that when a man does an action which has good consequences from a bad motive, we may nevertheless think badly of him for it. And it may be admitted that, in some cases at least, it is right and proper that a man's motives should thus influence our judgement. But the question is: What *sort* of moral judgement is it right and proper that they should influence? Should it influence our view as to whether the action in question is right or wrong? It seems very doubtful whether, as a rule, it actually does affect our judgement on this particular point, for we are quite accustomed to judge that a man sometimes acts *wrongly* from the best of motives; and though we should admit that the good motive forms some excuse, and that the whole state of things is better than if he had done the same thing from a bad motive, it yet does not lead us to deny that the action *is* wrong. There is, therefore, reason to think that the kind of moral judgements which a consideration of motives actually *does* affect do not consist of judgements as to whether the action done from the motive is *right* or *wrong;* but are moral judgements *of some different kind;* and there is still more reason to think that it is only judgements of some different kind which *ought* to be influenced by it.

The fact is that judgements as to the rightness and wrongness of actions are by no means the only kind of moral judgements which we make; and it is, I think, solely because some of these other judgements are confused with judgements of right and wrong that the latter are ever held to depend upon the motive. There are three other kinds of judgements which are chiefly concerned in this case. In the first place it may be held that some motives are *intrinsically good* and others *intrinsically bad;* and though this is a view which is inconsistent with the theory of our first two chapters, it is not a view which we are at present concerned to dispute: for it is not at all inconsistent with the principle which we are at present considering— namely, that right and wrong always depend solely upon consequences. If we held this view, we might still hold that a man may act wrongly from a good motive, and rightly from a bad one, and that the motive would make no difference whatever to the rightness or wrongness of the action. What it would make a difference to is the goodness or badness of the whole state of affairs: for, if we suppose the same action to be done in one case from a good motive and in the other from a bad one, then, so far as the consequences of the action are concerned, the goodness of the whole state of things will be the same, while the presence of the good motive will mean the presence of an *additional* good in the one case which is absent in the other. For this reason alone, therefore, we might justify the view that motives are relevant to *some* kinds of moral judgements, though not to judgements of right and wrong.

And there is yet another reason for this view, and this a reason which may be consistently held even by those who hold the theory of our first two chapters. It may be held, namely, that good motives have a *general* tendency to produce right conduct, though they do not *always* do so, and bad motives to produce wrong conduct; and this would be another reason which would justify us in regarding right actions done from a good motive differently from right actions done from a bad one. For though, in the case supposed, the bad motive would not *actually* have led to wrong action, yet, if it is true that motives of that kind do *generally* lead to wrong action, we should be right in passing this judgement upon it; and judgements to the effect that a motive is of a kind which generally leads to wrong action are undoubtedly moral judgements of a sort, and an important sort, though they do not prove that every action done from such a motive is wrong.

And finally motives seem also to be relevant to a third kind of moral judgement of great importance—namely, judgements as to whether, and in what degree, the agent *deserves* moral praise or blame for acting as he did. This question as to what is deserving of moral praise or blame is, I think, often confused with the question as to what is right or wrong. It is very natural, at first sight, to assume that to call an action morally praiseworthy is the same thing as to say that it is right, and to call it morally blameworthy the same thing as to say that it is wrong. But yet a very little reflection suffices to show that the two things are certainly distinct. When we say that an action *deserves* praise or blame, we imply that it is *right* to praise or blame it; that is to say, we are making a judgement *not* about the rightness of the original action, but about the rightness of the further action which we should take, if we praised or blamed it. And these two judgements are certainly not identical; nor is there any reason to think that what is right *always* also deserves to be praised, and what is wrong *always* also deserves to be blamed. Even, therefore, if the motive *is* relevant to the question whether an action deserves praise or blame, it by no means follows that it is *also* relevant to the question whether it is right or wrong. And there is some reason to think that the motive *is* relevant to judgements of the former kind: that we really *ought* sometimes to praise an action done from a bad motive less than if it had been done from a good one, and to blame an action done from a good motive less than if it had been done from a bad one. For one of the considerations upon which the question whether it is right to blame an action depends, is that our blame may tend to prevent the agent from doing similar wrong actions in future; and obviously, if the agent only acted wrongly from a motive which is not likely to lead him wrong in the future, there is less need to try to deter him by blame than if he had acted from a motive which was likely to lead him to act wrongly again. This is, I think, a very real reason why we *sometimes* ought to blame a man less when he does wrong from a good motive. But I do not mean to say that the question whether a man deserves moral praise or blame, or the degree to which he deserves it, depends *entirely* or *always* upon his motive. I think it certainly does not. My point is only that this *question* does *sometimes* depend on the motive in some degree; whereas the question whether his action was right or wrong *never* depends upon it at all.

There are, therefore, at least three different kinds of moral judgements, in making which it is at least plausible to hold that we ought to take account of motives; and if all these judgements are carefully distinguished from that particular kind which is solely concerned with the question whether an action is right or wrong, there ceases, I think, to be any reason to suppose that this last question ever depends upon the motive at all. At all events the mere fact that motives are and ought to be taken account of in *some* moral judgements does not constitute such a reason. And hence this fact cannot be urged as an objection to the view that right and wrong depend solely on consequences.

But there remains one last objection to this view, which is, I am inclined to think, the most serious of all. This is an objection which will be urged by people who strongly maintain that right and wrong do *not* depend either upon the nature of the action or upon its motive, and who will even go so far as to admit as self-evident the hypothetical proposition that *if* any being absolutely *knew* that one action would have better total consequences than another, then it *would* always be his duty to choose the former rather than the latter. But what such people would point out is that this hypothetical case is hardly ever, if ever, realized among us men. We hardly ever, if ever, *know for certain* which among the courses open to us *will* produce the best consequences. Some accident, which we could not possibly have foreseen, may always falsify the most careful calculations, and make an action, which we had every reason to think would have the best results, *actually* have worse ones than some alternative would have had. Suppose, then, that a man has taken all possible care to assure himself that a given course will be the best, and has adopted it for that reason, but that owing to some subsequent event, which he could not possibly have foreseen, it turns out *not* to be the best: are we for that reason to say that his action was wrong? It may seem outrageous to say so; and yet this is what we must say, if we are to hold that right and wrong depend upon the *actual* consequences. Or suppose that a man has deliberately chosen a course, which he has every reason to suppose will *not* produce the best consequences, but that some unforeseen accident defeats his purpose and makes it actually turn out to be the best: are we to say that such a man, because of this unforeseen accident, has acted rightly? This also may seem an outrageous thing to say; and yet we must say it, if we are to hold that right and wrong depend upon the *actual* consequences. For these reasons many people are strongly inclined to hold that they do *not* depend upon the *actual* consequences, but only upon those which were antecedently *probable,* or which the agent had *reason* to expect, or which it was *possible* for him to *foresee.* They are inclined to say that an action is *always* right, whatever its *actual* consequences may be, provided the agent had reason to expect that they would be the best possible; and *always* wrong, if he had reason to expect that they would not.

This, I think, is the most serious objection to the view that right and wrong depend upon the *actual* consequences. But yet I am inclined to think that even this objection can be got over by reference to the distinction between what is right or wrong, on the one hand, and what is morally praiseworthy or blameworthy on the other. What we should naturally say of a man whose action turns out badly owing to some unforeseen accident when he had every reason to expect that it would turn out well, is not that his action was right, but rather that *he is not to blame.* And it may be fully admitted that in such a case he really *ought* not to be blamed; since blame cannot possibly serve any good purpose, and would be likely to do harm. But, even if we admit that he was not to blame, is that any reason for asserting also that he acted rightly? I cannot see that it is; and therefore I am inclined to think that in all such cases the man really did act *wrongly,* although he is not to blame, and although, perhaps, he even deserves praise for acting as he did.

But the same difficulty may be put in another form, in which there may seem an even stronger case against the view that right and wrong depend on the *actual* consequences. Instead of considering what judgement we ought to pass on an action *after* it has been done, and when many of its results are already known, let us consider what judgement we ought to pass on it *beforehand,* and when the question is which among several courses still open to a man he *ought* to choose. It is admitted that he cannot *know for certain* beforehand which of them will actually have the best results; but let us suppose that he has every reason to think that one of them will produce decidedly better results than any of the others—that all probability is in favour of this view. Can we not say, in such a case, that he absolutely *ought* to choose that one? that he will be acting very *wrongly* if he chooses any other? We certainly *should* actually say so; and many people may be inclined to think that we should be right in saying so, no matter what the results may subsequently prove to be. There does seem to be a certain paradox in maintaining the opposite: in maintaining that, in such a case, it can possibly be true that he *ought* to choose a course, which he has every reason to think will *not* be the best. But yet I am inclined to think that even this difficulty is not fatal to our view. It may be admitted that we should say, and should be justified in saying, that he absolutely *ought* to choose the course, which he has reason to think will be the best. But we may be justified in saying many things, which we do not know to be true, and which in fact are not so, provided there is a strong probability that they are. And so in this case I do not see why we should not hold, that though we should be justified in saying that he *ought* to choose one course, yet it may not be really true that he ought. What certainly will be true is that he will deserve the strongest moral blame if he does not choose the course in question, even though it may be wrong. And we are thus committed to the paradox that a man may really deserve the strongest moral condemnation for choosing an action, which *actually* is right. But I do not see why we should not accept this paradox.

I conclude, then, that there is no conclusive reason against the view that our theory is right, so far as it maintains that the question whether an action is right or wrong *always* depends on its *actual* consequences. There seems no sufficient reason for holding either that it depends on the intrinsic nature of the action, or that it depends upon the motive, or even that it depends on the *probable* consequences.

VI   FREE WILL

Throughout the last three chapters we have been considering various objections which might be urged against the theory stated in Chapters I and II. And the very last objection which we considered was one which consisted in asserting that the question whether an action is right or wrong does *not* depend upon its *actual* consequences, because whenever the consequences, *so far as the agent can foresee,* are *likely* to be the best possible, the action is always right, even if they are not *actually* the best possible. In other words, this objection rested on the view that right and wrong depend, in a sense, upon what the agent *can know.* And in the present chapter I propose to consider objections, which rest, instead of this, upon the view that right and wrong depend upon what the agent *can do.*

Now it must be remembered that, *in a sense,* our original theory does hold and even insists that this is the case. We have, for instance, frequently referred to it in the last chapter as holding that an action is only right, if it produces the best *possible* consequences; and by 'the best *possible* consequences' was meant 'consequences at least as good as would have followed from any action which the agent *could* have done instead'. It does, therefore, hold that the question whether an action is right or wrong does always depend upon a comparison of its consequences with those of all the other actions which the agent *could* have done instead. It assumes, therefore, that wherever a voluntary action is right or wrong (and we have throughout only been talking of *voluntary* actions), it is true that the agent *could,* in a sense, have done something else instead. This is an absolutely essential part of the theory.

But the reader must now be reminded that all along we have been using the words 'can', 'could', and 'possible' *in a special sense.* It was explained in Chapter I (pp. 12-13), that we proposed, purely for the sake of brevity, to say that an agent *could* have done a given action, which he didn't do, wherever it is true that he could have done it, *if* he had chosen; and similarly by what he *can* do, or what is *possible,* we have always meant merely what is possible, *if* he chooses. Our theory, therefore, has not been maintaining, after all, that right and wrong depend upon what the agent absolutely *can* do, but only on what he can do, *if* he chooses. And this makes an immense difference. For, by confining itself in this way, our theory avoids a controversy, which cannot be avoided by those who assert that right and wrong depend upon what the agent absolutely *can* do. There are few, if any, people who will *expressly* deny that we very often really could, *if* we had chosen, have done something different from what we actually did do. But the moment it is asserted that any man ever absolutely *could* have done anything other than what he did do, there are many people who *would* deny this. The view, therefore, which we are to consider in this chapter—the view that right and wrong depend upon what the agent absolutely *can* do—at once involves us in an extremely difficult controversy—the controversy concerning Free Will. There are many people who strenuously deny that any man ever *could* have done anything other than what he actually did do, or ever *can* do anything other than what he *will* do; and there are others who assert the opposite equally strenuously. And whichever view be held is, if *combined* with the view that right and wrong depend upon what the agent absolutely *can* do, liable to contradict our theory very seriously. Those who hold that no man ever *could* have done anything other than what he did do, are, if they *also* hold that right and wrong depend upon what we *can* do, logically bound to hold that no action of ours is ever right and none is ever wrong; and this is a view which is, I think, often actually held, and which, of course, constitutes an extremely serious and fundamental objection to our theory: since our theory implies, on the contrary, that we very often do act *wrongly,* if never quite rightly. Those, on the other hand, who hold that we absolutely *can* do things, which we don't do, and that right and wrong depend upon what we thus *can* do, are also liable to be led to contradict our theory, though for a different reason. Our theory holds that, provided a man could have done something else, *if* he had chosen, that is sufficient to entitle us to say that his action really is either right or wrong. But those who hold the view we are considering will be liable to reply that this is by no means sufficient: that to say that it *is* sufficient, is entirely to misconceive the nature of right and wrong. They will say that, in order that an action may be *really* either right or wrong, it is absolutely essential that the agent should have been *really able* to act differently, able in some sense quite other than that of merely being able, *if* he had chosen. *If* all that were really ever true of us were merely that we could have acted differently, *if* we had chosen, then, these people would say, it really would be true that none of our actions are ever right and that none are ever wrong. They will say, therefore, that our theory entirely misses out one absolutely essential condition of right and wrong—the condition that, for an action to be right or wrong, it must be *freely* done. And moreover, many of them will hold also that the class of actions which we absolutely *can* do is often not identical with those which we can do, *if* we choose. They may say, for instance, that very often an action, which we *could* have done, *if* we had chosen, is nevertheless an action which we *could not* have done; and that an action is always right, if it produces as good consequences as any other action which we really *could* have done instead. From which it will follow that many actions which our theory declares to be *wrong*, will, according to them, be right, because these actions really are the best of all that we *could* have done, though *not* the best of all that we could have done, *if* we had chosen.

Now these objections seem to me to be the most serious which we have yet had to consider. They seem to me to be serious because (1) it is very difficult to be sure that right and wrong do not really depend, as they assert, upon what we *can* do and not merely on what we can do, *if* we choose; and because (2) it is very difficult to be sure in what sense it is true that we ever *could* have done anything different from what we actually did do. I do not profess to be sure about either of these points. And all that I can hope to do is to point out certain facts which do seem to me to be clear, though they are often overlooked; and thus to isolate clearly for the reader's decision, those questions which seem to me to be really doubtful and difficult.

Let us begin with the question: Is it ever true that a man *could* have done anything else, except what he actually did do? And, first of all, I think I had better explain exactly how this question seems to me to be related to the question of Free Will. For it is a fact that, in many discussions about Free Will, this precise question is never mentioned at all; so that it might be thought that the two have really nothing whatever to do with one another. And indeed some philosophers do, I think, definitely imply that they *have* nothing to do with one another: they seem to hold that our wills can properly be said to be free even if we *never* can, in any sense at all, do anything else except what, in the end, we actually do do. But this view, if it is held, seems to me to be plainly a mere abuse of language. The statement that we have Free Will is certainly ordinarily understood to imply that we really sometimes have the power of acting differently from the way in which we actually do act; and hence, if anybody tells us that we have Free Will, while at the same time he means to deny that we ever have such a power, he is simply misleading us. We certainly have *not* got Free Will, in the ordinary sense of the word, if we never really *could*, in any sense at all, have done anything else than what we did do; so that, in this respect, the two questions certainly are connected. But, on the other hand, the mere fact (if it is a fact) that we sometimes *can*, in *some* sense, do what we don't do, does not necessarily entitle us to say that we *have* Free Will. We certainly *haven't* got it, *unless* we can; but it doesn't follow that we *have* got it, even if we *can*. Whether we have or not will depend upon the precise sense in which it is true that we can. So that even if we do decide that we really *can* often, in *some* sense, do what we don't do, this decision by itself does not entitle us to say that we have Free Will.

And the first point about which we can and should be quite clear is, I think, this: namely, that we certainly often *can*, in *some* sense, do what we don't do. It is, I think, quite clear that this is so; and also very important that we should realize that it is so. For many people are inclined to assert, quite without qualification: No man ever *could*, on any occasion, have done anything else than what he actually did do on that occasion. By asserting this quite simply, without qualification, they imply, of course (even if they do not mean to imply), that there is *no* proper sense of the word 'could', in which it is true that a man *could* have acted differently. And it is this implication which is, I think, quite certainly absolutely false. For this reason, anybody who asserts, without qualification, 'Nothing ever *could* have happened, except what actually did happen', is making an assertion which is quite unjustifiable, and which he himself cannot help constantly contradicting. And it is important to insist on this, because many people do make this unqualified assertion, without seeing how violently it contradicts what they themselves, and all of us, believe, and rightly believe, at other times. If, indeed, they insert a qualification—if they merely say. 'In *one* sense of the word *"could"* nothing ever *could* have happened, except what did happen', then, they may perhaps be perfectly right: we are not disputing that they may. All that we are maintaining is that, in *one* perfectly proper and legitimate sense of the word 'could', and that one of the very commonest senses in which it is used, it is quite certain that some things which didn't happen *could* have happened. And the proof that this is so, is simply as follows.

It is impossible to exaggerate the frequency of the occasions on which we *all* of us make a distinction between two things, neither of which *did* happen—a distinction which we express by saying, that whereas the one *could* have happened, and other could *not*. No distinction is commoner than this. And no one, I think, who fairly examines the instances in which we make it, can doubt about three things: namely (1) that very often there really is *some* distinction between the two things, corresponding to the language which we use; (2) that this distinction, which really *does* subsist between the things, is *the* one which we mean to express by saying that the one was possible and the other impossible; and (3) that this way of expressing it is a perfectly proper and legitimate way. But if so, it absolutely follows that one of the commonest and most legitimate usages of the phrases 'could' and 'could not' is to express a difference, which often really does hold between two things *neither* of which did actually happen. Only a few instances need be given. I *could* have walked a mile in twenty minutes this morning, but I certainly could *not* have run two miles in five minutes. I did not, *in fact,* do either of these two things; but it is pure nonsense to say that the mere fact that I *did* not, does away with the distinction between them, which I express by saying that the one *was* within my powers, whereas the other was *not*. *Although* I did neither, yet the one was certainly *possible* to me in a sense in which the other was totally *im*possible. Or, to take another instance: It is true, as a rule, that cats *can* climb trees, whereas dogs *can't*. Suppose that on a particular afternoon neither A's cat nor B's dog *do* climb a tree. It is quite absurd to say that this mere fact proves that we must be wrong if we say (as we certainly often should say) that the cat *could* have climbed a tree, though she didn't, whereas the dog *couldn't*. Or, to take an instance which concerns an inanimate object. Some ships *can* steam 20 knots, whereas others *can't* steam more than 15. And the

mere fact that, on a particular occasion, a 20-knot steamer *did* not
actually run at this speed certainly does not entitle us to say that she
could not have done so, in the sense in which a 15-knot one *could*
not. On the contrary, we all can and should distinguish between
cases in which (as, for instance, owing to an accident to her propel-
ler) she did not, *because* she could not, and cases in which she did
not, *although* she *could*. Instances of this sort might be multiplied
quite indefinitely; and it is surely quite plain that we all of us do
continually use such language: we continually, when considering
two events, neither of which *did* happen, distinguish between them
by saying that whereas the one *was* possible, though it didn't happen,
the other was *im*possible. And it is surely quite plain that what we
mean by this (whatever it may be) is something which is often perfectly true. But, if so, then anybody who asserts, without qualification,
'Nothing ever *could* have happened, except what did happen', is
simply asserting what is false.

It is, therefore, quite certain that we often *could* (in *some* sense)
have done what we did not do. And now let us see how this fact is
related to the argument by which people try to persuade us that it is
not a fact.

The argument is well known: it is simply this. It is assumed (for
reasons which I need not discuss) that absolutely everything that
happens has a *cause* in what precedes it. But to say this is to say that
it follows *necessarily* from something that preceded it; or, in other
words, that, once the preceding events which are its cause had happened, it was absolutely *bound* to happen. But to say that it was
bound to happen, is to say that nothing else *could* have happened
instead; so that, if *everything* has a cause, *nothing* ever could have
happened except what did happen.

And now let us assume that the premise of this argument is correct: that everything really *has* a cause. What really follows from it?
Obviously all that follows is that, in *one* sense of the word 'could',
nothing ever *could* have happened, except what did happen. This
really *does* follow. But, *if* the word 'could' is ambiguous—if, that is to
say, it is used in different senses on different occasions—it is obviously
quite possible that though, in *one* sense, nothing ever could have
happened except what did happen, yet in *another* sense, it may at
the same time be perfectly true that some things which did not
happen *could* have happened. And can anybody undertake to assert
with certainty that the word 'could' is *not* ambiguous? that it may not

have more than one legitimate sense? *Possibly* it is not ambiguous; and, *if* it is not, then the fact that some things, which did not happen, *could* have happened, really would contradict the principle that everything has a cause; and, in that case, we should, I think, have to give up this principle, because the fact that we often *could* have done what we did not do, is so certain. But the assumption that the word 'could' is *not* ambiguous is an assumption which certainly should not be made without the clearest proof. And yet I think it often is made, without any proof at all; simply because it does not occur to people that words often are ambiguous. It is, for instance, often assumed, in the Free Will controversy, that the question at issue is solely as to whether everything is caused, or whether acts of will are sometimes uncaused. Those who hold that we *have* Free Will, think themselves bound to maintain that acts of will some-times have *no* cause; and those who hold that everything is caused think that this proves completely that we have not Free Will. But, in fact, it is extremely doubtful whether Free Will is at all incon-sistent with the principle that everything is caused. Whether it is or not, all depends on a very difficult question as to the meaning of the word 'could'. All that is certain about the matter is (1) that, if we have Free Will, it must be true, in *some* sense, that we sometimes *could* have done, what we did not do; and (2) that, if everything is caused, it must be true, in *some* sense, that we *never could* have done, what we did not do. What is very *un*certain, and what certainly needs to be investigated, is whether these two meanings of the word 'could' are the same.

Let us begin by asking: What is the sense of the word 'could', in which it is so certain that we often *could* have done, what we did not do? What, for instance, is the sense in which I *could* have walked a mile in twenty minutes this morning, though I did not? There is one suggestion, which is very obvious: namely, that what I mean is simply after all that I could, *if* I had chosen; or (to avoid a possible complication) perhaps we had better say 'that I *should, if* I had chosen'. In other words, the suggestion is that we often use the phrase 'I *could*' simply and solely as a short way of saying 'I *should, if* I had chosen'. And in all cases, where it is certainly true that we *could* have done, what we did not do, it is, I think, very difficult to be quite sure that this (or something similar) is *not* what we mean by the word 'could'. The case of the ship may seem to be an excep-tion, because it is certainly not true that she would have steamed twenty knots if *she* had chosen; but even here it seems possible that what we mean is simply that she *would, if the men on board of her* had chosen. There are certainly good reasons for thinking that we *very often* means by 'could' merely 'would, if so and so had chosen'. And if so, when we have a sense of the word 'could' in which the fact that we often *could* have done what we did not do, is perfectly compatible with the principle that everything has a cause: for to say that, *if* I had performed a certain act of will, I should have done something which I did not do, in no way contradicts this principle.

And an additional reason for supposing that this *is* what we often mean by 'could', and one which is also a reason why it is important to insist on the obvious fact that we very often really *should* have acted differently, *if* we had willed differently, is that those who deny that we ever *could* have done anything, which we did not do, often speak and think as if this really did involve the conclusion that we never should have acted differently, even *if* we had willed differently. This occurs, I think, in two chief instances—one in reference to the future, the other in reference to the past. The first occurs when, because they hold that nothing *can* happen, except what *will* happen, people are led to adopt the view called Fatalism—the view that *whatever we will,* the result will always be the same; that it is, therefore, *never* any use to make one choice rather than another. And this conclusion will really follow if by 'can' we mean '*would* happen, even *if* we were to will it'. But it is certainly untrue, and it certainly does not follow from the principle of causality. On the contrary, reasons of exactly the same sort and exactly as strong as those which lead us to suppose that everything has a cause, lead to the conclusion that if we choose one course, the result will *always* be different in *some* respects from what it would have been, if we had chosen another; and we know also that the difference would *sometimes* consist in the fact that *what* we chose would come to pass. It is certainly often true of the future, therefore, that whichever of two actions we *were* to choose, *would* actually be done, although it is quite certain that only one of the two *will* be done.

And the second instance, in which people are apt to speak and think, as if, *because* no man ever *could* have done anything but what he did do, it follows that he would not, even *if* he had chosen, is as follows. Many people seem, in fact, to conclude directly from the first of these two propositions, that we can never be justified in praising or blaming a man for anything that he does, or indeed for making any distinction between what is right or wrong, on the one hand, and what is lucky or unfortunate on the other. They conclude, for instance, that there is never any reason to treat or to regard the voluntary commission of a crime in any different way from that in which we treat or regard the involuntary catching of a disease. The man who committed the crime *could* not, they say, have helped committing it any more than the other man could have helped catching the disease; both events were equally inevitable; and though both may of course be great *misfortunes,* though both may have very bad consequences and equally bad ones—there is no justification whatever, they say, for the distinction we make between them when we say that the commission of the crime was *wrong,* or that the man was morally to blame for it, whereas the catching of the disease was *not* wrong and the man was not to blame for it. And this conclusion, again, will really follow if by 'could not' we mean 'would not, even if he had willed to avoid it'. But the point I want to make is, that it follows *only* if we make this assumption. That is to say, the mere fact that the man *would* have succeeded in avoiding the crime, *if* he had chosen (which is certainly often true), whereas the other man would *not* have succeeded in avoiding the disease, *even* if he had chosen (which is certainly also often true) gives an ample justification for regarding and treating the two cases differently. It gives such a justification, because, where the occurrence of an event *did* depend upon the will, there, by acting on the will (as we may do by blame or punishment) we have often a reasonable chance of preventing similar events from recurring in the future; whereas, where it did *not* depend upon the will, we have no such chance. We may, therefore, fairly say that those who speak and think, as if a man who brings about a misfortune *voluntarily* ought to be treated and regarded in exactly the same way as one who brings about an equally great misfortune *involuntarily,* are speaking and thinking *as if* it were not true that we ever should have acted differently, even *if* we had willed to do so. And that is why it is extremely important to insist on the absolute certainty of the fact that we often really *should* have acted differently, *if* we had willed differently.

There is, therefore, much reason to think that when we say we *could* have done a thing which we did not do, we *often* mean merely that we *should* have done it, *if* we had chosen. And if so, then it is quite certain that, in *this* sense, we often really *could* have done what we did not do, and that this fact is in no way inconsistent with the principle that everything has a cause. And for my part I must confess that I cannot feel certain that this may not be *all* that we usually mean and understand by the assertion that we have Free Will; so that those who deny that we have it are really denying (though, no doubt, often unconsciously) that we ever *should* have acted differently, even if we had willed differently. It has been sometimes held that this *is* what we mean; and I cannot find any conclusive argument to the contrary. And if it is what we mean, then it absolutely follows that we really *have* Free Will, and also that this fact is quite consistent with the principle that everything has a cause; and it follows also that our theory will be perfectly right, when it makes right and wrong depend on what we *could* have done, *if* we had chosen.

But, no doubt, there are many people who will say that this is *not* sufficient to entitle us to say that we have Free Will; and they will say this for a reason, which certainly has some plausibility, though I cannot satisfy myself that it is conclusive. They will say, namely: Granted that we often *should* have acted differently, *if* we had chosen differently, yet it is not true that we have Free Will, unless it is *also* often true in such cases that we *could* have *chosen* differently. The question of Free Will has been thus represented as being merely the question whether we ever *could* have chosen, what we did not choose, or ever *can* choose, what, in fact, we shall not choose. And since there is some plausibility in this contention, it is, I think, worth while to point out that here again it is absolutely certain that, in two different senses, at least, we often *could* have chosen, what, in fact, we did not choose; and that in neither sense does this fact contradict the principle of causality.

The first is simply the old sense over again. If by saying that we *could* have done, what we did not do, we often mean merely that we *should* have done it, *if* we had chosen to do it, then obviously, by saying that we *could* have *chosen* to do it, we may mean merely that we *should* have so chosen, *if* we had chosen *to make the choice*. And I think there is no doubt it is often true that we should have chosen to do a particular thing *if* we had chosen to make the choice; and that this is a very important sense in which it is often in our power to make a choice. There certainly is such a thing as making an effort to induce ourselves to *choose* a particular course; and I think there is no doubt that often if we *had* made such an effort, we *should* have made a choice, which we did not in fact make.

And besides this, there is another sense in which, whenever we have several different courses of action in view, it is *possible* for us to choose any one of them; and a sense which is certainly of some practical importance, even if it goes no way to justify us in saying that we have Free Will. This sense arises from the fact that in such cases we can hardly ever *know for certain* beforehand, *which* choice we actually *shall* make; and one of the commonest senses of the word 'possible' is that in which we call an event 'possible' when no man can *know for certain* that it will *not* happen. It follows that almost, if not quite always, when we make a choice, after considering alternatives, it *was* possible that we should have chosen one of these alternatives, which we did not actually choose; and often, of course, it was not only possible, but highly probable, that we should have done so. And this fact is certainly of practical importance, because many people are apt much too easily to assume that it is quite certain that they *will not* make a given choice, which they know they ought to make, if it were possible; and their belief that they *will* not make it tends, of course, to prevent them from making it. For this reason it is important to insist that they can hardly ever know for certain with regard to any given choice that they will *not* make it.

It is, therefore, quite certain (1) that we often *should* have *acted* differently, if we had chosen to; (2) that similarly we often should have *chosen* differently, *if* we had chosen so to choose; and (3) that it was almost always *possible* that we should have chosen differently, in the sense that no man could know for certain that we should *not* so choose. All these three things are facts, and all of them are quite consistent with the principle of causality. Can anybody undertake to say for certain that none of these three facts and *no* combination of them will justify us in saying that we have Free Will? Or, suppose it granted that we have not Free Will, unless it is often true that we *could* have chosen, what we did not choose:—Can any defender of Free Will, or any opponent of it, show conclusively that what he means by '*could* have chosen' in this proposition, is anything different from the two certain facts, which I have numbered (2) and (3), or some combination of the two? Many people, no doubt, will still insist that these two facts alone are by no means sufficient to entitle us to say that we have Free Will: that it must be true we were *able* to choose, in some quite other sense. But nobody, so far as I know, has ever been able to tell us exactly what that sense is. For my part, I can find no conclusive argument to show either that some such other sense of 'can' is necessary, or that it is not. And, therefore, this chapter must conclude with a doubt. It is, I think, possible that, instead of saying, as our theory said, that an action is only right, when it produces consequences as good as any which would have followed from any other action which the agent *would* have done, *if* he had chosen, we should say instead that it is right whenever and only when the agent *could not have done* anything which would have produced better consequences: and that this *'could not* have done' is *not* equivalent to 'would not have done, *if* he had chosen', but is to be understood in the sense, whatever it may be, which is sufficient to entitle us to say that we have Free Will. If so, then our theory would be wrong, just to this extent.

VII INTRINSIC VALUE

The main conclusions, at which we have arrived so far with regard to the theory stated in Chapters I and II, may be briefly
summed up as follows. I tried to show, first of all, (1) that to say
that a voluntary action is *right,* or *ought* to be done, or is *wrong,* is
not the same thing as to say that any being or set of beings whatever, either human or non-human, has towards it any mental attitude
whatever—either an attitude of feeling, or of willing, or of thinking
something about it; and that hence no proof to the effect that any
beings, human or non-human, have any such attitude towards an
action is sufficient to show that it is right, or ought to be done, or is
wrong; and (2) similarly, that to say that any one thing or state of
things is *intrinsically good,* or *intrinsically bad,* or that one is *intrin-*
sically better than another, is also not the same thing as to say that
any being or set of beings has towards it any mental attitude whatever—either an attitude of feeling, or of desiring, or of thinking something about it; and hence that here again no proof to the effect that
any being or set of beings *has* some such mental attitude towards
a given thing or state of things is ever sufficient to show that it is
intrinsically good or bad. These two points are extremely important,
because the contrary view is very commonly held, in some form or
other, and because (though this is not always seen), whatever form
it be held in, it is absolutely fatal to one or both of two very fundamental principles, which our theory implies. In many of their forms
such views are fatal to the principle (1) that no action is ever *both*
right and wrong; and hence also to the view that there is any characteristic whatever which *always* belongs to right actions and *never* to

wrong ones; and in *all* their forms they are fatal to the principle, (2) that if it is once the duty of any being to do an action whose total effects will be A rather than one whose total effects will be B, it must *always* be the duty of any being to do an action whose total effects will be precisely similar to A rather than one whose total effects will be precisely similar to B, if he has to choose between them.

I tried to show, then, first of all, that these two principles may be successfully defended against this first line of attack—the line of attack which consists in saying (to put it shortly) that 'right' and 'good' are merely *subjective* predicates. But we found next that even those who admit and insist (as many do) that 'right' and 'intrinsically good' are *not* subjective predicates, may yet attack the second principle on another ground. For this second principle implies that the question whether an action is right or wrong must always depend upon its *actual* consequences; and this view is very commonly disputed on one or other of three grounds, namely (1) that it sometimes depends merely on the *intrinsic nature* of the action, or, in other words, that certain kinds of actions would be absolutely always right, and others absolutely always wrong, *whatever* their consequences might be, or (2) that it depends, partly or wholly, on the *motive* from which the action is done, or (3) that it depends on the question whether the agent had *reason to expect* that its consequences would be the best possible. I tried, accordingly, to show next that each of these three views is untrue.

But, finally, we raised, in the last chapter, a question as to the *precise* sense in which right and wrong do *depend* upon the actual consequences. And here for the first time we came upon a point as to which it seemed very doubtful whether our theory was right. All that could be agreed upon was that a voluntary action is right whenever and only when its total consequences are *as* good, intrinsically, as any that would have followed from any action which the agent *could have* done instead. But we were unable to arrive at any certain conclusion as to the precise sense in which the phrase 'could have' must be understood if this proposition is to be true; and whether, therefore, it *is* true, if we give to these words the precise sense which our theory gave to them.

I conclude, then, that the theory stated in Chapters I and II is right so far as it merely asserts the three principles (1) That there *is* some characteristic which belongs and must belong to absolutely *all* right voluntary actions and to *no* wrong ones; (2) That one such characteristic consists in the fact that the total consequences of right actions must always be as good, intrinsically, as any which it was *possible* for the agent to produce under the circumstances (it being uncertain, however, in what sense precisely the word 'possible' is to be understood), whereas this can never be true of wrong ones; and (3) That if any set of consequences A is once intrinsically better than another set B, any set precisely similar to A must always be intrinsically better than a set precisely similar to B. We have, indeed, not considered all the objections which might be urged against these three principles; but we have, I think, considered all those which are most commonly urged, *with one single exception*. And I must now briefly state what this one remaining objection is, before I go on to point out the respect in which this theory, which was stated in Chapters I and II, seems to me to be utterly wrong, in spite of being right as to all these three points.

This one last objection may be called the objection of Egoism; and it consists in asserting that no agent can ever be under any obligation to do the action, whose *total* consequences will be the best possible, *if* its total effects upon *him*, personally, are not the best possible; or in other words that it always would be *right* for an agent to choose the action whose total effects *upon himself* would be the best, even if *absolutely all* its effects (taking into account its effects on other beings as well) would *not* be the best. It asserts in short that it can never be the duty of any agent to sacrifice his own good to the general good. And most people, who take this view, are, I think, content to assert this, without asserting further that it must always be his positive *duty* to prefer his own good to the general good. That is to say, they will admit that a man may be acting *rightly*, even if he *does* sacrifice his own good to the general good; they only hold that he will be acting *equally* rightly, if he does *not*. But there are some philosophers who seem to hold that it must *always* be an agent's positive duty to do what is best for *himself—always*, for instance, to do what will conduce most to his own 'perfection', or his own salvation, or his own 'self-realization'; who imply, therefore, that it would be his duty so to act, even if the action in question did *not* have the best possible consequences upon the whole.

Now the question, whether this view is true, in either of these two different forms, would, of course, be of no practical importance, if it were true that, as a matter of fact, every action which most promotes the general good always *also* most promotes the agent's own good, and vice versa. And many philosophers have taken great pains to try to show that this *is* the case: some have even tried to show that it *must* necessarily be the case. But it seems to me that none of the arguments which have been used to prove this proposition really do show that it is by any means *universally* true. A case, for instance, may arise in which, if a man is to secure the best consequences for the world as a whole, it may be absolutely necessary that he should sacrifice his own life. And those who maintain that, even in such a case, he will absolutely always be securing the greatest possible amount of good *for himself*, must either maintain that in some future life he will receive goods sufficient to compensate him for all that he might have had during many years of continued life in this world—a view to which there is the objection that it may be doubted, whether we shall have any future life at all, and that it is even more doubtful, what, *if* we shall, that life will be like; or else they must maintain the following paradox.

Suppose there are two men, A and B, who up to the age of thirty have lived lives of equal intrinsic value; and that at that age it becomes the duty of each of them to sacrifice his life for the general good. Suppose A does his duty and sacrifices his life, but B does not, and continues to live for thirty years more. Those who hold that the agent's own good *always* coincides with the general good, must then hold that B's sixty years of life, no matter how well the remaining thirty years of it may be spent, cannot possibly have so much intrinsic value as A's thirty years. And surely this is an extravagant paradox, however much intrinsic value we may attribute to those final moments of A's life in which he does his duty at the expense of his life; and however high we put the loss in intrinsic value to B's life, which arises from the fact that, in this one instance, he failed to do his duty. B may, for instance, repent of this one act and the whole of the remainder of his life may be full of the highest goods; and it seems extravagant to maintain that all the goods there may be in this last thirty years of it cannot possibly be enough to make his life more valuable, intrinsically, than that of A.

I think, therefore, we must conclude that a maximum of true good, for ourselves, is by no means always secured by those actions which are necessary to secure a maximum of true good for the world as a whole; and hence that it *is* a question of practical importance, whether, in such cases of conflict, it is always a duty, or right, for us to prefer our own good to the general good. And this is a question which, so far as I can see, it is impossible to decide by argument one way or the other. If any person, after clearly considering the question, comes to the conclusion that he can never be under any obligation to sacrifice his own good to the general good, if they *were* to conflict, or even that it would be wrong for him to do so, it is, I think, impossible to prove that he is mistaken. But it is certainly equally impossible for him to prove that he is not mistaken. And, for my part, it seems to me quite self-evident that he is mistaken. It seems to me quite self-evident that it must always be our duty to do what will produce the best effects *upon the whole,* no matter how bad the effects upon ourselves may be and no matter how much good we ourselves may lose by it.

I think, therefore, we may safely reject this last objection to the principle that it must always be the duty of every agent to do that one, among all the actions which he *can* do on any given occasion, whose *total consequences* will have the greatest intrinsic value; and we may conclude, therefore, that the theory stated in Chapters I and II is right as to all the three points yet considered, except for the doubt as to the precise sense in which the words 'can do' are to be understood in this proposition. But obviously on any theory which maintains, as this one does, that right and wrong depend on the intrinsic value of the consequences of our actions, it is extremely important to decide rightly what kinds of consequences *are* intrinsically better or worse than others. And it is on this important point that the theory in question seems to me to take an utterly wrong view. It maintains, as we saw in Chapter II, that any whole which contains *more pleasure* is always intrinsically better than one which contains less, and that none can be intrinsically better, *unless* it contains more pleasure; it being remembered that the phrase 'more pleasure', in this statement, is not to be understood as meaning strictly what it says, but as standing for any one of five different alternatives, the nature of which was fully explained in our first two chapters. And the last question we have to raise is, therefore: Is this proposition true or not? and if not, what *is* the right answer to the question: What kinds of things are intrinsically better or worse than others?

And first of all it is important to be quite clear as to how this question is related to another question, which is very liable to be confused with it: namely the question whether the proposition which was distinguished in Chapter I, as forming *the first part* of the theory there stated, is true or not: I mean, the proposition that quantity of pleasure is a correct *criterion* of right and wrong, or that, *in this world,* it always is, *as a matter of fact,* our duty to do the action which will produce a maximum of pleasure, or (for this is, perhaps, more commonly held) to do the action which, *so far as we can see,* will produce such a maximum. This latter proposition has been far more often *expressly* held than the proposition that what contains more pleasure is *always* intrinsically better than what contains less; and many people may be inclined to think they are free to maintain it, even if they deny that the intrinsic value of every whole is *always* in proportion to the quantity of pleasure it contains. And so, *in a sense,* they are; for it is quite possible, *theoretically,* that quantity of pleasure should always be a correct *criterion* of right and wrong, here in this world, even if intrinsic value is not always in exact proportion to quantity of pleasure. But though this is theoretically possible, it is, I think, easy to see that it is extremely *unlikely* to be the case. For if it were the case, what it would involve is this. It would involve our maintaining that, where the total consequences of any actual voluntary action have more intrinsic value than those of the possible alternatives, it *absolutely always* happens to be true that they *also* contain more pleasure, although, in other cases, we know that degree of intrinsic value is by no means always in proportion to quantity of pleasure contained. And, of course, it is theoretically possible that this should be so: it is *possible* that the total consequences of actual voluntary actions should form a complete exception to the general rule: that, in their case, what has more intrinsic value should *absolutely always* also contain more pleasure, although, in other cases, this is by no means always true: but anybody can see, I think, that, in the absence of strict proof that it is so, the probabilities are all the other way. It is, indeed, so far as I can see, quite impossible absolutely to *prove* either that it is so or that it is not so; because *actual* actions in this world are liable to have such an immense number of indirect and remote consequences, which we cannot trace, that it is impossible to be quite certain how the *total* consequences of any two actions will compare either in respect of intrinsic value, or in respect of the quantity of pleasure they contain. It *may,* therefore, *possibly* be the case that quantity of pleasure *is,* as a matter of fact, a correct *criterion* of right and wrong, even if intrinsic value is *not* always in proportion to quantity of pleasure contained. But it is impossible to *prove* that it is a correct criterion, except by assuming that intrinsic value always *is* in proportion to quantity of pleasure. And most of those who have held the former view have, I think, in fact made this assumption, even if they have not definitely realized that they were making it.

Is this assumption true, then? Is it true that one whole will be intrinsically better than another, whenever and only when it contains more pleasure, no matter what the two may be like in other respects? It seems to me almost impossible that any one, who fully realizes the consequences of such a view, can possibly hold that it *is* true. It involves our saying, for instance, that a world in which absolutely nothing except pleasure existed—no knowledge, no love, no enjoyment of beauty, no moral qualities—must yet be intrinsically better—better worth creating—provided only the total quantity of pleasure in it were the least bit greater, than one in which all these things existed *as well as* pleasure. It involves our saying that, even if the total quantity of pleasure in each was exactly equal, yet the fact that all the beings in the one possessed in addition knowledge of many different kinds and a full appreciation of all that was beautiful or worthy of love in their world, whereas *none* of the beings in the other possessed any of these things, would give us no reason whatever for preferring the former to the latter. It involves our saying that, for instance, the state of mind of a drunkard, when he is intensely pleased with breaking crockery, is just as valuable, in itself—just as well worth having, as that of a man who is fully realizing all that is exquisite in the tragedy of King Lear, provided only the mere quantity of pleasure in both cases is the same. Such instances might be multiplied indefinitely, and it seems to me that they constitute a *reductio ad absurdum* of the view that intrinsic value is always in proportion to quantity of pleasure. Of course, here again, the question is quite incapable of proof either way. And if anybody, after clearly considering the issue, does come to the conclusion that no one kind of enjoyment is ever intrinsically better than another, provided only that the pleasure in both is equally intense, and that, if we *could* get as much pleasure in the world, without needing to have any knowledge, or any moral qualities, or any sense of beauty, as we can get *with* them, then all these things would be entirely superfluous, there is no way of proving that he is wrong. But it seems to me almost impossible that anybody, who does really get the question clear, should take such a view; and, if anybody were to, I think it is self-evident that he would be wrong.

It may, however, be asked: If the matter is as plain as this, how has it come about that anybody ever has adopted the view that intrinsic value *is* always in proportion to quantity of pleasure, or has ever argued, as if it were so? And I think one chief answer to this question is that those who have done so have *not* clearly realized all the consequences of their view, partly because they have been too exclusively occupied with the particular question as to whether, in the case of *the total consequences* of *actual* voluntary actions, degree of intrinsic value is not always in proportion to quantity of pleasure—a question which, as has been admitted, is, in itself, much more obscure. But there is, I think, another reason, which is worth mentioning, because it introduces us to a principle of great importance. It may, in fact, be held, with great plausibility, that no whole can ever have any intrinsic value *unless* it contains some pleasure; and it might be thought, at first sight, that this reasonable, and perhaps true, view could not possibly lead to the wholly unreasonable one that intrinsic value is always *in proportion* to quantity of pleasure: it might seem obvious that to say that nothing can be valuable *without* pleasure is a very different thing from saying that intrinsic value is always *in proportion* to pleasure. And it is, I think, in fact true that the two views are really as different as they seem, and that the latter does not at all follow from the former. But, if we look a little closer, we may, I think, see a reason why the latter should very naturally have been *thought* to follow from the former.

The reason is as follows. If we say that no whole can ever be intrinsically good, *unless* it contains some pleasure, we are, of course, saying that if from any whole, which is intrinsically good, we were to subtract all the pleasure it contains, the remainder, whatever it might be, would have no intrinsic goodness at all, but must always be either intrinsically *bad*, or else intrinsically indifferent: and this (if we remember our definition of intrinsic value) is the same thing as to say that this remainder actually *has* no intrinsic goodness at all, but always *is* either positively bad or indifferent. Let us call the pleasure which such a whole contains, A, and the whole remainder, whatever it may be, B. We are then saying that the whole A+B is intrinsically good, but that B is *not* intrinsically good at all. Surely it seems to follow that the intrinsic value of A+B cannot possibly be greater than that of A by itself? How, it may be asked, could it possibly be otherwise? How, by adding to A something, namely B, which has *no* intrinsic goodness at all, could we possibly get a whole which has *more* intrinsic value than A? It may naturally seem to be self-evident that we could not. But, if so, then it absolutely follows that we can never increase the value of any whole whatever except by adding *pleasure* to it: we may, of course, *lessen* its value, by adding other things, e.g. by adding pain; but we can never *increase* it except by adding pleasure.

Now from this it does not, of course, follow strictly that the intrinsic value of a whole is always *in proportion* to the quantity of pleasure it contains in the special sense in which we have throughout been using this expression—that is to say, as meaning that it is in proportion to the *excess* of pleasure over pain, in one of the five senses explained in Chapter I. But it is surely very natural to think that it does. And it *does* follow that we must be wrong in the reasons we gave for disputing this proposition. It does follow that we must be wrong in thinking that by adding such things as knowledge or a sense of beauty to a world which contained a certain amount of pleasure, without adding any more pleasure, we could increase the intrinsic value of that world. If, therefore, we are to dispute the proposition that intrinsic value *is* always in proportion to quantity of pleasure we must dispute this argument. But the argument may seem to be almost indisputable. It has, in fact, been used as an argument in favour of the proposition that intrinsic value *is* always in proportion to quantity of pleasure, and I think it has probably had much influence in inducing people to adopt that view, even if they have not expressly put it in this form.

How, then, can we dispute this argument? We might, of course, do so, by rejecting the proposition that no whole can ever be intrinsically good, *unless* it contains some pleasure; but, for my part, though I don't feel certain that this proposition *is* true, I also don't feel at all certain that it is *not* true. The part of the argument which it seems to me certainly can and ought to be disputed is another part—namely, the assumption that, where a whole contains two factors, A and B, and one of these, B, has no intrinsic goodness at all, the intrinsic value of the whole cannot be *greater* than that of the other factor, A. This assumption, I think, obviously rests on a still more general assumption, of which it is only a special case. The general assumption is: That where a whole consists of two factors A and B, the amount by which its intrinsic value exceeds that of one of these two factors must always be equal to that of the other factor. Our special case will follow from this general assumption: because it will follow that if B be intrinsically *indifferent,* that is to say, if its intrinsic value=o, then the amount by which the value of the whole A+B exceeds the value of A must also=o, that is to say, the value of the whole must be precisely *equal* to that of A; while if B be intrinsically *bad,* that is to say, if its intrinsic value is less than o, then the amount by which the value of A+B will exceed that of A will also be less than o, that is to say, the value of the whole will be *less* than that of A. Our special case does then follow from the general assumption; and nobody, I think, would maintain that the special case was true without maintaining that the general assumption was also true. The general assumption may, indeed, very naturally seem to be self-evident: it has, I think, been generally assumed that it is so: and it may seem to be a mere deduction from the laws of arithmetic. But, so far as I can see, it is *not* a mere deduction from the laws of arithmetic, and, so far from being self-evident, is certainly untrue.

Let us see exactly what we are saying, if we deny it. We are saying that the fact that A and B *both* exist together, together with the fact that they have to one another any relation which they do happen to have (when they exist together, they always must have *some* relation to one another; and the precise nature of the relation certainly may in some cases make a great difference to the value of the whole state of things, though, perhaps, it need not in all cases)—that these two facts *together* must have a certain amount of intrinsic value, that is to say must be either intrinsically good, or intrinsically bad, or intrinsically indifferent, and that the amount by which this value exceeds the value which the existence of A would have, if A existed quite alone, *need* not be equal to the value which the existence of B would have, if B existed quite alone. This is all that we are saying. And can any one pretend that such a view necessarily contradicts the laws of arithmetic? or that it is self-evident that it cannot be true? I cannot see any ground for saying so; and if there is no ground, then the argument which sought to show that we can never add to the value of any whole *except* by adding pleasure to it, is entirely baseless.

If, therefore, we reject the theory that intrinsic value is always in proportion to quantity of pleasure, it does seem as if we may be compelled to accept the principle that *the amount by which the value of a whole exceeds that of one of its factors is not necessarily equal to that of the remaining factor*—a principle which, if true, is very important in many other cases. But, though at first sight this principle may seem paradoxical, there seems to be no reason why we should not accept it; while there are other independent reasons why we should accept it. And, in any case, it seems quite clear that the degree of intrinsic value of a whole is *not* always in proportion to the quantity of pleasure it contains.

But, if we do reject this theory, what, it may be asked, can we substitute for it? How can we answer the question, what kinds of consequences are intrinsically better or worse than others?

We may, I think, say, first of all, that for the same reason for which we have rejected the view that intrinsic value is always in proportion to quantity of pleasure, we must also reject the view that it is always in proportion to the quantity of any other *single* factor whatever. Whatever single kind of thing may be proposed as a measure of intrinsic value, instead of pleasure—whether knowledge, or virtue, or wisdom, or love—it is, I think, quite plain that it is not such a measure; because it is quite plain that, however valuable any one of these things may be, we may always add to the value of a whole which contains any one of them, not only by adding more of that one, but also *by adding something else instead*. Indeed, so far as I can see, there is no characteristic whatever which always distinguishes every whole which has greater intrinsic value from every whole which has less, *except* the fundamental one that it would always be the duty of every agent to prefer the better to the worse, if he had to choose between a pair of actions, of which they would be the *sole* effects. And similarly, so far as I can see, there is no characteristic whatever which belongs to all things that are intrinsically *good* and only to them—except simply the one that they all *are* intrinsically good and *ought* always to be preferred to *nothing at all,* it we had to choose between an action whose sole effect would be one of them and one which would have no effects whatever. The fact is that the view which seems to me to be true is the one which, apart from theories, I think every one would naturally take, namely, that there are an *immense variety* of different things, *all* of which are intrinsically good; and that though all these things may perhaps have some characteristic *in common,* their variety is so great that they have none, which, *besides* being common to them all, is also *peculiar* to them—that is to say, which never belongs to anything which is intrinsically bad or indifferent. All that can, I think, be done by way of making plain what kinds of things are intrinsically good or bad, and what are better or worse than others, is to classify some of the chief kinds of each, pointing out what the factors are upon which their goodness or badness depends. And I think this is one of the most profitable things which can be done in Ethics, and one which has been too much neglected hitherto. But I have not space to attempt it here.

I have only space for two final remarks. The first is that there do seem to be two important characteristics, which are *common* to absolutely all intrinsic goods, though not peculiar to them. Namely (1) it does seem as if nothing can be an intrinsic good unless it contains *both* some feeling and *also* some other form of consciousness; and, as we have said before, it seems possible that amongst the feelings contained must always be some amount of pleasure. And (2) it does also seem as if every intrinsic good must be a complex whole containing a considerable variety of different factors—as if, for instance, nothing so simple as pleasure by itself, however intense, could ever be any good. But it is important to insist (though it is obvious) that neither of these characteristics is *peculiar* to intrinsic goods: they may obviously *also* belong to things bad and indifferent. Indeed, as regards the first, it is not only true that many wholes which contain both feeling and some other form of consciousness are intrinsically bad; but it seems also to be true that nothing can be intrinsically bad, *unless* it contains some feeling.

The other final remark is that we must be very careful to distinguish the two questions (1) whether, and in what degree, a thing is *intrinsically* good and bad, and (2) whether, and in what degree, it is capable of adding to or subtracting from the intrinsic value of a whole of which it forms a part, from a third, entirely different question, namely (3) whether, and in what degree, a thing is *useful* and has good *effects,* or *harmful* and has *bad* effects. All three questions are very liable to be confused, because, in common life, we apply the names 'good' and 'bad' to things of all three kinds indifferently: when we say that a thing is 'good' we may mean either (1) that it is intrinsically good or (2) that it adds to the value of many intrinsically good wholes or (3) that it is useful or has good effects; and similarly when we say that a thing is bad we may mean any one of the three corresponding things. And such confusion is very liable to lead to mistakes, of which the following are, I think, the commonest. In the first place, people are apt to assume with regard to things, which really are very good indeed in senses (1) or (2), that they are scarcely any good at all, simply because they do not seem to be of much *use*—that is to say, to lead to *further* good effects; and similarly, with regard to things which really are very bad in senses (1) or (2), it is very commonly assumed that there cannot be much, if any, harm in them, simply because they do not seem to lead to *further* bad results. Nothing is commoner than to find people asking of a good thing: What *use* is it? and concluding that, if it is no use, it cannot be any good; or asking of a bad thing: What harm does it do? and concluding that if it *does* no harm, there cannot be any harm *in* it. Or, again, by a converse mistake, of things which really are very useful, but are not good at all in senses (1) and (2), it is very commonly assumed that they *must* be good in one or both of these two senses. Or again, of things, which really are very good in senses (1) and (2), it is assumed that, because they are good, they cannot possibly do harm. Or finally, of things, which are neither intrinsically good nor useful, it is assumed that they cannot be any good at all, although in fact they are very good in sense (2). All these mistakes are liable to occur, because, in fact, the degree of goodness or badness of a thing in any one of these three senses is by no means always in proportion to the degree of its goodness or badness in either of the other two; but if we are careful to distinguish the three different questions, they can, I think, all be avoided.

INDEX